Windows 11 Made Easy

Getting Started and Making
It Work for You

Mike Halsey

Apress®

Windows 11 Made Easy: Getting Started and Making It Work for You

Mike Halsey
TERRES DE HAUTE CHARENTE, France

ISBN-13 (pbk): 978-1-4842-8034-8   ISBN-13 (electronic): 978-1-4842-8035-5
https://doi.org/10.1007/978-1-4842-8035-5

Managing Director, Apress Media LLC: Welmoed Spahr
Acquisitions Editor: Smriti Srivastava
Development Editor: Laura Berendson
Coordinating Editor: Shrikant Vishwakarma

Cover designed by eStudioCalamar

Cover image designed by Pexels

Distributed to the book trade worldwide by Springer Science+Business Media LLC, 1 New York Plaza, Suite 4600, New York, NY 10004. Phone 1-800-SPRINGER, fax (201) 348-4505, e-mail orders-ny@springer-sbm. com, or visit www.springeronline.com. Apress Media, LLC is a California LLC and the sole member (owner) is Springer Science + Business Media Finance Inc (SSBM Finance Inc). SSBM Finance Inc is a **Delaware** corporation.

For information on translations, please e-mail booktranslations@springernature.com; for reprint, paperback, or audio rights, please e-mail bookpermissions@springernature.com, or visit http://www.apress.com/ rights-permissions.

Apress titles may be purchased in bulk for academic, corporate, or promotional use. eBook versions and licenses are also available for most titles. For more information, reference our Print and eBook Bulk Sales web page at http://www.apress.com/bulk-sales.

Any source code or other supplementary material referenced by the author in this book is available to readers on GitHub via the book's product page, located at https://link.springer.com/book/ 10.1007/978-1-4842-8034-8.

Printed on acid-free paper

Table of Contents

About the Author

Mike Halsey is a recognized technical expert. He is the author of help and how-to books for Windows 7, 8, and 10, including accessibility, productivity, and troubleshooting. He is also the author of *The Green IT Guide* (Apress). Mike is well versed in the problems and issues that PC users experience when setting up, using, and maintaining their PCs and knows how difficult and technical it can appear.

He understands that some subjects can be intimidating, so he approaches each subject area in straightforward and easy-to-understand ways. Mike is originally from the UK, but now lives in the south of France with his rescue border collies, Evan and Robbie. You can contact Mike on Twitter at @MikeHalsey.

About the Technical Reviewer

Carsten Thomsen is a back-end developer primarily but working with smaller front-end bits as well. He has authored and reviewed a number of books and created numerous Microsoft Learning courses, all to do with software development. He works as a freelancer/contractor in various countries in Europe, using Azure, Visual Studio, Azure DevOps, and GitHub as some of the tools he works with. Being an exceptional troubleshooter, asking the right questions, including the less logical ones, in a most logical to least logical fashion, he also enjoys working with architecture, research, analysis, development, testing, and bug fixing. Carsten is a very good communicator with great mentoring and team-lead skills and great skills in researching and presenting new material.

Acknowledgments

With thanks to Andreas Stenhall MVP, for his assistance with this book.

CHAPTER 1

Finding Your Way Around Windows 11

It can be daunting when Microsoft release a new version of Windows, especially when, as they did with Windows 10 and now again with Windows 11, it's offered for free and is delivered to your PC by Windows Update. One day you're happily using Windows 10, and then the next morning, bleary-eyed and starting your first cup of coffee, you suddenly realize that everything is *not* where it used to be.

The Start button has moved, the Start Menu has changed, you don't know where all your apps are, and there's lots of new icons at the bottom of your screen and you have no idea what they are. Fear not weary traveler, as this is the book to bring you up to speed.

In fact, tell you what, let's do better than that. What I'll do, seeing as it's you, is to show you how to get the very best experience from Windows 11, whether you use it for play, shopping, work, or school.

I'll show you how to connect to your company systems so you can work from home. We'll look at how you can be more productive and get stuff done. I'll show you how to make Windows 11 easier to use for everybody from those who are colorblind to elderly parents with shaky hands, and we'll also get you connected to your Xbox and playing games online.

Most importantly though, I'll show you how to do all of this safely. You don't want to have to constantly worry about being infected with malware, or having your identity stolen, and you want to make sure too that Microsoft, Google, Facebook, Amazon, and all the other companies whose products and services you use on your PC aren't invading your personal privacy.

© Mike Halsey 2022
M. Halsey, *Windows 11 Made Easy*, https://doi.org/10.1007/978-1-4842-8035-5_1

Windows 11 Primer

Let's dive straight in with some of the most useful information about Windows 11 and what you'll need to know not just as you use your PC today, but for when you continue to use it into the future. You will have questions, so let's deal with them one at a time.

What Is Windows 11 Anyway?

Windows 11 is the evolution of Windows 10. In fact, it really *is* just the same as Windows 10; it just looks different. Underneath, Windows 10 and Windows 11 are exactly the same operating systems, so work and operate in the same way. This means that any apps and hardware that worked with Windows 10 are guaranteed to work with Windows 11.

Windows 10 Kept Changing, Will Windows 11?

Over its life, Windows 10 went through quite a few changes. You can see in Figure 1-1, which shows Windows 10's Settings panel when it was first launched in 2015 (left) and the Settings panel six years later in 2021 (right).

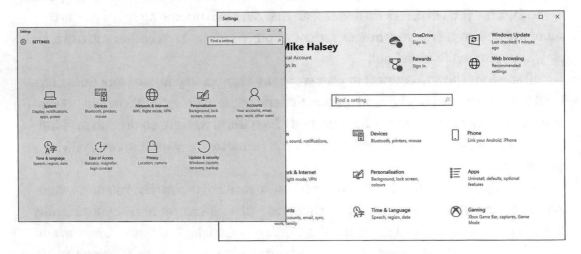

Figure 1-1. *Windows 10 changed quite a bit over its life*

The same will happen with Windows 11 over its life, and you might find that in a few years something I refer to in this book looks different than it does in the images here or is in a slightly different place. Don't worry though as, if this is likely to happen, I'll detail it in the chapter and show you how to find things that might have moved.

How Long Will Windows 11 Be Around For?

Another good question, as it was widely thought Windows 10 would be the last major version of the operating system. In fairness, this was a quote from a Microsoft executive at a conference back in 2015, but Microsoft never actually said it themselves in a formal way. It wasn't in a blog post, it wasn't in a press announcement, but because they never said the quote was wrong either, everybody just assumed it was true.

In late 2019, Microsoft began working on a new version of Windows called Windows 10 X. This was intended to make the PC experience significantly more secure and used advanced technologies to create what was intended to be the future of modern computing, but they could never get it working in a reliable way. As part of that development though, they devised a new look for Windows and, not wanting to waste it, decided to launch Windows 11 to give the PC market a bit of a kick-start as the world started to come out of the pandemic.

Officially, Windows 11 will be supported for about ten years, meaning you can be certain of continuing using it until 2031, but we don't have an exact date yet. Each *Feature Pack* for Windows 11, which I'll talk about in a minute, will be supported for two years, and then you'll have to upgrade to the latest feature pack.

Okay, What's a Feature Pack?

A Feature Pack (we used to call them Service Packs) are the big updates to Windows. These bring all the new features and sometimes a few changes to the operating system. They're not like the stability, security, and cumulative updates you get, which are there to keep Windows stable and secure.

Microsoft will release a Feature Pack once a year, usually in the autumn (fall for those in the United States). These will be delivered to you automatically, but if you'd rather wait and see if there are any problems with the first releases (as there can sometimes be), I'll show you how to do this in Chapter 11.

Why Do I Have to Use a Microsoft Account?

This is the elephant in the room, and lots of people are unhappy with it. We use accounts to sign into everything these days – a Facebook account to sign into Facebook, Instagram, or WhatsApp, an Amazon account to shop online, a Google or an Apple account to get our smartphones working, and a Microsoft Account to sign into Windows – but is it worth it on your PC?

Some people are "old-school" and just have a stand-alone PC sitting in a corner of the living room or spare room, on which you type documents, do calculations on spreadsheets, do a little online banking, and do some shopping. This is fine if you only ever have one PC, don't really keep Internet bookmarks for websites, have all your passwords written down or use a password manager like LastPass, and keep a regular backup copy of your files and documents on other devices.

Where a Microsoft Account comes in useful is both for automatically saving all your files, documents, and photos to Microsoft's OneDrive cloud backup service and for synchronizing all your documents, photos, settings, website logins and passwords, Internet bookmarks, and more, not just between all your PCs, but your smartphone too if you use the Microsoft Edge web browser on it.

This is also useful should your PC need replacing, as everything will be automatically resynced to your new desktop PC or laptop.

If you want to use a local account instead, you will need a copy of Windows 11 Pro. You can search in Settings, in *System* ➤ *About* to see which version you have, see Figure 1-2, and I'll show you how to find settings later in this chapter.

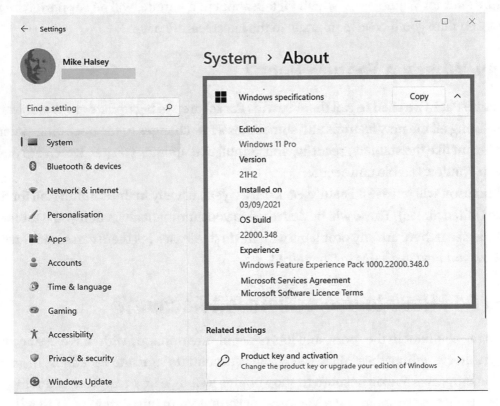

Figure 1-2. *You need Windows 11 Pro to use a local account*

If you're concerned about privacy and security though, don't be. In Chapter 9, I'll show you how to configure and manage your privacy in Windows 11.

Let's Get Started!

When you start Windows 11, you'll first get to what's called the Lock Screen, see Figure 1-3. This is where you'll be asked for your password or pin. (I'll show you how to set these up and how to use a fingerprint reader or your webcam to sign in automatically in Chapter 9.)

Figure 1-3.   *The Lock Screen is the first thing you see in Windows 11*

In the front and center is your picture (sometimes called an avatar) and a box in which you can type your password or pin code. Below that is/are options to change how you sign in, that is, switching between a password, pin, and Windows Hello via your camera.

In the bottom left are buttons for all the user accounts on your PC. You will only see this if there is more than one account on the PC, and I'll show you how to add and manage accounts for your family and other people in Chapter 2.

In the bottom right are buttons for connecting to a Wi-Fi network, open the *Ease of Access* settings (which I'll detail in full in Chapter 6), and then there's a button in the bottom-right corner to either restart or shut down the PC.

The Windows 11 Desktop and Start Menu

Once you're past the Lock Screen, you'll see the new Windows 11 desktop. It's a little different from previous versions of Windows, but this is because improvements have been made.

The first thing you'll notice is that the Start button is no longer in the far-left corner of the Taskbar (the colored bar that runs along the bottom of the screen), but don't worry as if you want it put back there, I'll show you how in Chapter 2.

Clicking the Start button opens the new Start Menu, see Figure 1-4, and this too has changed, so let's take a couple of minutes looking around the desktop and Start Menu to see what's what and what's where.

Figure 1-4. *The desktop and Start Menu have changed slightly in Windows 11*

As we've already seen, the Start button and your icons for pinned and open apps can now be found in the center of the Taskbar. Any app that's open will have a blue dot underneath it, and the app that's currently in use (sometimes called in focus) on the desktop will have a blue line, see Figure 1-5.

Figure 1-5. *Taskbar icons and the Start button now sit in the center of your screen*

At the right side of the Taskbar are two areas. One is called the *System Tray*, and it displays icons you might need for running apps (like OneDrive or your antivirus software) and for Windows features such as connecting to a Wi-Fi network or changing the volume, see Figure 1-6.

Figure 1-6. *The System Tray sits on the right side of the Taskbar*

To their left is a small up arrow (^) which you can click to display hidden icons. Any hidden icon that's important to you can be dragged back to the Taskbar to always show it, and any you don't need can be dragged onto the arrow to hide them.

At the right end of the Taskbar is the clock, date, and notification icon. If you have any notifications, as seen in Figure 1-6, there will be a small circle with a number in it. Clicking this icon or the clock will pop up a panel on the right of your screen with notifications at the top and your calendar below, see Figure 1-7. I will show you how to manage notifications later in this chapter.

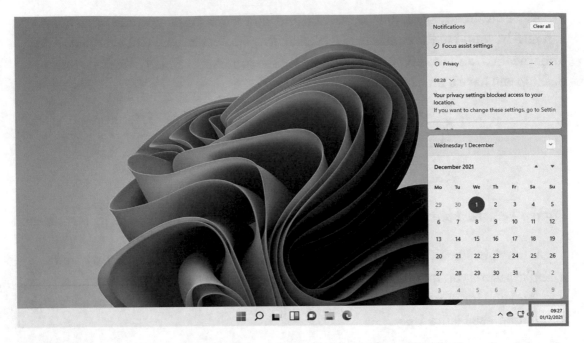

Figure 1-7. *You can display your notifications by clicking the clock to the right of the Taskbar*

Then we move to the Start Menu, which has four main sections. At the very top of the Start Menu is a search box. You can type in here to search for everything from your installed apps to files, documents, pictures, and any music of video files you have on the PC, and you can even search the Internet from here, see Figure 1-8. I will show you how to use search later in this chapter.

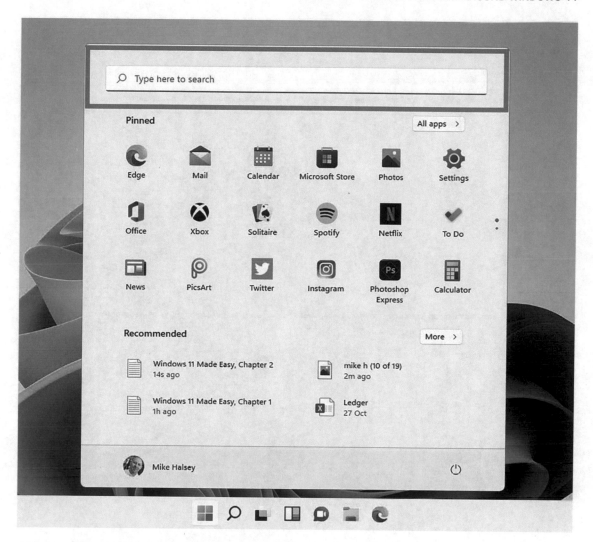

Figure 1-8. *You can search for anything from the Start Menu*

Below this is the list of your pinned apps, you can change these, and I will show you how later in the chapter. In the top right of this section is an *All apps* button that you can click to display a scrollable list of all the apps installed on your PC, see Figure 1-9.

Figure 1-9. *You access your pinned and installed apps from the Start Menu*

Below the apps list is a section called *Recommended* (note this may get a different name in a future update to Windows 11), and this is where you'll see a list of all your most recently used and accessed files and documents, see Figure 1-10. This can make it really easy to find that document you were working on yesterday.

Figure 1-10. *Your most recently used documents will appear in the Start Menu*

If you have a lot of recent files and documents, you will also see a *More* button in the top-right corner of this section. You can click this to display a complete list of all the files and documents you have accessed most recently. I will show you more about managing files and documents in Chapter 5.

Lastly, at the bottom of the Start Menu are two buttons. On the left is your user avatar. You can click this to switch between different user accounts on the PC if you have more than one, lock the PC if you're going away from it for a while (perhaps to lunch), and access your account settings, which we will look at in Chapter 2, see Figure 1-11.

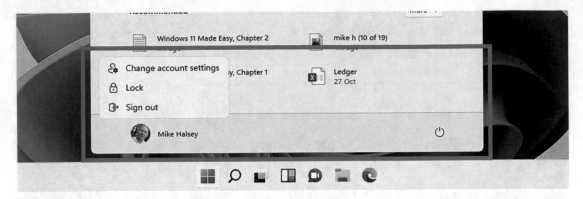

Figure 1-11. *You can sign out of your account and restart the PC from the Start Menu*

In the bottom-right corner of the Start Menu is a power button, and clicking this will display options to shut down and restart the PC, as well as putting it into a sleep state.

Running and Finding Apps

Windows 11 comes with a lot of apps already installed, including Microsoft Office, and apps for playing music and video. Many are pinned to the Start Menu already and all of them are available by clicking the *All apps* button as I detailed earlier.

You can move apps around in the Start Menu by dragging their icon with your mouse or finger (if your PC has a touch screen) to arrange them how you like. Right-clicking (touching and holding with your finger) an icon will display a menu of options. These include unpinning the app from the Start menu if you don't want to see if there, pinning it to the Taskbar instead (more on this in Chapter 7), or uninstalling it, see Figure 1-12.

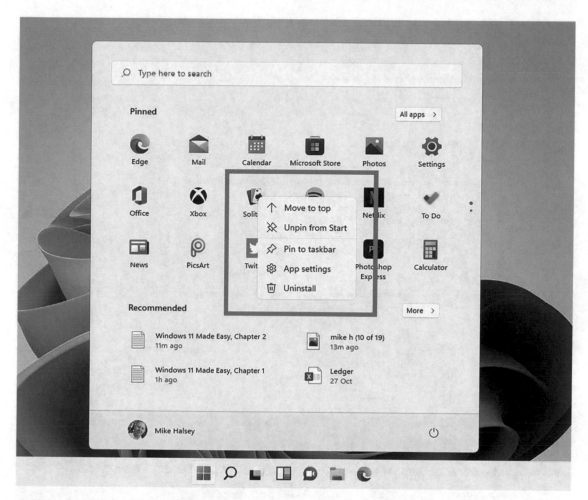

Figure 1-12. *You can right-click an app icon to get rid of it*

When you're in the *All apps* view, you can also right-click (touch and hold) an app to display a menu of options which include pinning it to the Start Menu and uninstalling it, see Figure 1-13.

Figure 1-13. *The all apps view allows you to pin apps to the Start Menu*

The Microsoft Store

If you open the *Microsoft Store* icon from the Start Menu, you'll find this a good place to install apps from. You might remember the Store first appeared in Windows 8, but the amount and the quality of the apps available were poor. With Windows 10 this didn't improve, but with Windows 11 things have changed.

The Microsoft Store in Windows 11 allows plug-in stores from other companies like Steam and Amazon, the latter of which brings with it support for Android apps, the ones that you will use on your phone or tablet. Note that this isn't the full Google Play Store, but rather a reduced version of it, but many popular Android apps will be available there. I'll talk about how to install and manage apps, including Android apps in full, in Chapter 4.

Figure 1-14. *The Microsoft Store is a good place to get apps*

Tip   One of the things that *could* change over time is the support for the full Google Play Store. While this is by no means certain, the details you'll find in Chapter 4 for installing the Amazon Android store can also be used to see if the Google Play Store is there too… you never know, we might get lucky one day!

Searching for Apps, Files, and More

You can search in Windows 11 direct from the Start Menu as I detailed earlier. You can either click in the search box at the top of the Start Menu and type or press the Windows key on your keyboard to open the Start Menu and then just start typing anyway. There is also a Search icon on the Taskbar to the right of the Start button you can press.

When you type, the search will begin automatically, see Figure 1-15. You will see under the search box the words *All*, *Apps*, *Documents*, *Web*, and *More*. You can click these to narrow your search to particular and specific items. By default, though the search results will show a mixture of all these things, with what Windows believes are the most relevant search results listed first.

Figure 1-15. *Search is easy to use in Windows 11*

Using Touch Controls

While we're on the subject of typing things, you might be using a Microsoft Surface or other touch screen device and either want or need to use the on-screen (virtual) keyboard.

In Windows 11, the icon for this will automatically appear when you do not have a keyboard attached, but you can manually configure it by right-clicking (touching and holding) anywhere in a blank area of the Taskbar and from the pop-up that appears, selecting *Taskbar Settings*, see Figure 1-16.

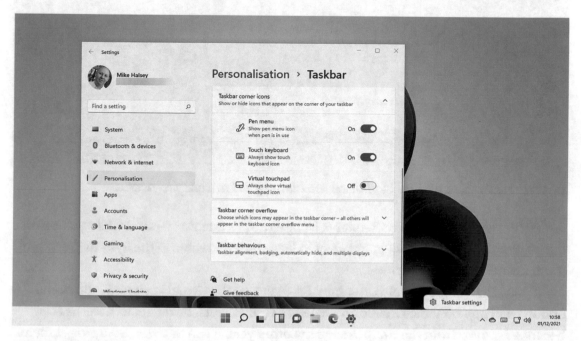

Figure 1-16. *The Taskbar settings allow you to display icons for the virtual keyboard and touchpad*

These icons will appear in the System Tray, and you can click them to display both the on-screen keyboard and the virtual touchpad, see Figure 1-17.

Figure 1-17. *The virtual keyboard and touchpad are easy to access*

I will detail these fully in Chapter 6, but there are a couple of useful tricks you can use the keyboard for, and so you might want to leave its icon visible in the System Tray even if you don't have a touch screen.

If you click (tap) and hold on some of the keys on the virtual keyboard, additional options will appear which include international characters. If you need these, as I do because I moved from the UK to France the other year, it can be a quick way to get them, see Figure 1-18.

Figure 1-18. *You can access international characters from the virtual keyboard*

While we're still on the subject of on-screen keyboards and international characters, you can also press the *Windows key + period* (.) on your keyboard to display the emoji panel (the virtual keyboard has a button for the emoji panel in its top-left corner if you're using a touch screen only). You can do this at any time and within any app.

This emoji panel as it's become known has buttons across the top for your most recently used characters; emojis; animated gifs (short, animated pictures); old-style emojis (still very popular in countries like China and Japan); international, currency, mathematics, and scientific symbols; and your cut and copy clipboard history, see Figure 1-19.

Figure 1-19. *The emoji panel can be used to access all types of content*

Finding Your Files and Documents

Being able to type on your PC isn't much good if you can't find any of your files and documents, but fortunately Microsoft have made this easy and the *File Explorer* icon is already pinned to your Taskbar. It looks like a yellow manila folder, and clicking it will display the main File Explorer panel, see Figure 1-20.

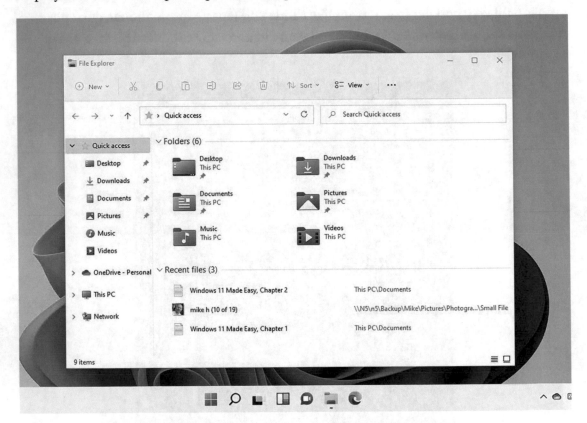

Figure 1-20. *File Explorer is where you can access files and documents*

I will show you how to really get to grips with File Explorer in Chapter 5, and there are some useful tips and tricks that can help make you really productive. In its normal form though, you will see colored folders both in the left-side panel and in the center of the window for your *Desktop, Downloads, Documents, Pictures, Music*, and *Videos*.

If you have signed into your Windows 11 PC using a Microsoft Account and have your files and documents stored in Microsoft's OneDrive cloud backup and sync service, you will see all of your files and documents already there for you to access, and I will show you how to set up and manage OneDrive in Chapter 5.

You can open your files and folders by double-clicking them with your mouse (tapping with your finger), but other options are available to you. The menu at the top of the File Explorer window contains *Sort* and *View* buttons. These allow you to change how files, documents, and folders are displayed. For example, you might want your most recent files and documents shown first, or want bigger icons, or more details about the files shown, see Figure 1-21.

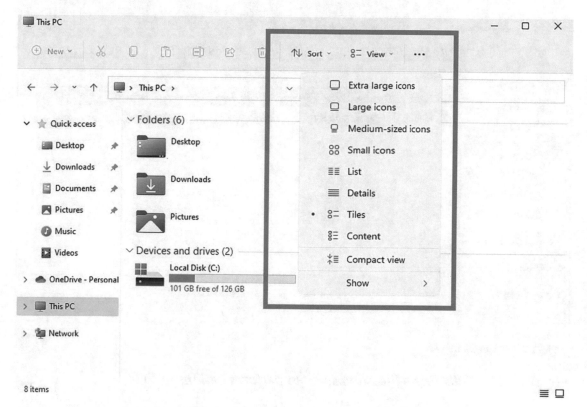

Figure 1-21. *You can change how files and documents are displayed in File Explorer*

At the left side of the menu bar is a *New* button, and you can click this to create new folders and documents in the currently displayed folder. These options will change depending on what apps you have installed, so you won't, for example, see *New Spreadsheet* as an option if you don't have a spreadsheet software like Microsoft Excel installed on the PC.

When you select a file or document by clicking or touching it, additional options will appear on the menu bar at the top of the File Explorer window, see Figure 1-22. These options will allow you to *cut* (when moving the file to a different disk or folder), *copy, rename, share,* and *delete* the selected item.

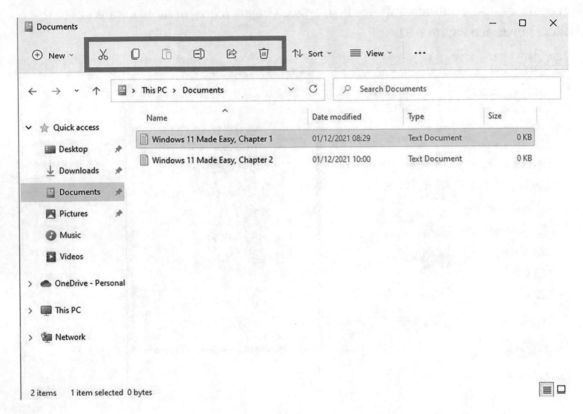

Figure 1-22. *Selecting a file allows you to perform actions with it*

Managing Notifications

You'll probably be used to getting notifications on your smartphone, and they also exist in Windows 11. They tell you when something happens, like an email or WhatsApp message has been received, or tell you that an update is available.

I showed you how to open the notification center at the beginning of this chapter, by clicking the notification icon in the bottom-right corner of the screen or by clicking the clock, see Figure 1-23.

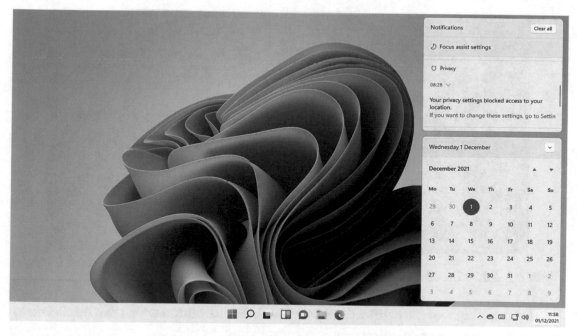

Figure 1-23. *Notifications appear on the right side of your screen*

Notifications appear above the calendar in a panel. Depending on the size of your screen, you might see a scroll bar so you can move up and down in the list. Each notification has a couple of options available when you hover your cursor over it.

The option on the right is a cross (x) which can be used to dismiss the notification, but if you want more control, such as to dismiss all notifications of that type, click the three dots icon (…) and you will be able to perform actions such as permanently dismissing all notifications of that type, or making them a higher priority, see Figure 1-24.

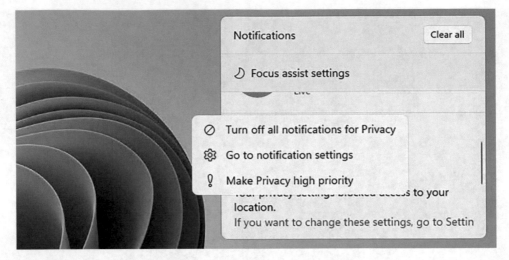

Figure 1-24. *You can get more control over notifications*

In the top right of the notifications panel is a *Clear all* button which can be clicked to remove all your current notifications.

Quick Settings

Next to the clock on the Taskbar, you will see icons for your network connection (either showing you're connected to a wired or a wireless network) and a speaker icon where you can control the volume of sound on your PC.

Clicking these icons will display the Quick Settings panel, see Figure 1-25. The icons you see here will vary, depending on how your PC is set up, but this is where you will see activation buttons for various Windows functions, such as activating a *Night Light*, where blue light is eliminated from your display to help prevent eyestrain, and access *Accessibility* settings.

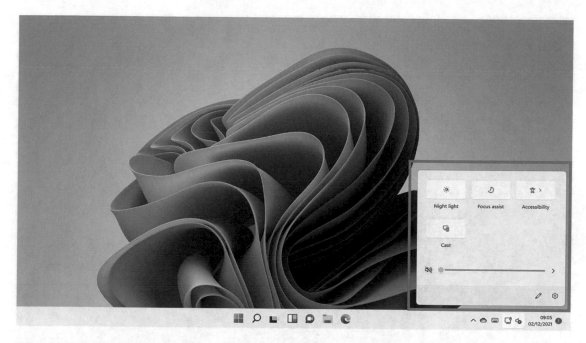

Figure 1-25. *Quick Settings buttons can pop up from the Taskbar*

Additionally, this is where you will see a volume slider, so that you can control the volume of music, video, and sounds from your PC. We will look at all of the quick settings options in much more detail throughout this book.

Switching Between and Closing Apps

When you have several apps open at a time, you will want to switch between them. There are different ways to do this, the first being clicking the icon on the Taskbar for the running app you want to use. Additionally, you can use the *Task View* icon, which are the black and gray overlapping squares that sit to the right of the Start button.

This will display images of all your running apps, and you can click one to switch to it, see Figure 1-26. Additionally, there are options at the bottom of this screen to create a *New desktop*, and we will look at how you can use this to separate different tasks, like work and gaming, in Chapter 7.

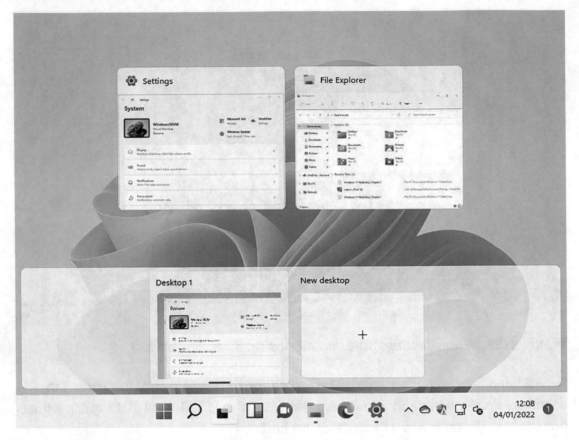

Figure 1-26. *Task View can be used to switch between running apps*

Tip   If you want a really quick way to switch between running apps, and are using a keyboard, press the *Windows key + Tab* to display all your running apps, and then keep pressing Windows key + Tab until the app you want to switch to is highlighted. Releasing the keys will then switch you to that running app.

Additionally, when you hover your mouse over one of the apps displayed in Task View, a red *Close* button will appear in its top-right corner. You can also close apps by right-clicking (tap and hold) their icon on the Taskbar where you will also find a close option.

Tip   Every window has three icons in its top-right corner; they are, from left to right, *Minimize* (to leave the app running but remove it from your screen), *Maximize* (to make the app fill all of your screen), and *Close* (to exit and close the running app).

Summary

These are all subjects for future chapters, and we're going to kick-start straight into one of those, as in the next chapter we'll look at how you can customize how Windows 11 looks and feels; how you can set up and manage user accounts, including keeping children safe online and with games; and how you can get started online by getting your email and other online accounts working.

CHAPTER 2

Personalizing Windows 11

Windows 11 is very easy on the eye, but that doesn't mean it's not really easy to personalize how it looks and make it more to your own liking. There can be good reasons for this too, such as making text on your screen easier to read and even reducing the power consumption of your laptop or tablet.

Settings is also where you can add, remove, and manage accounts on your PC, for everything from your email, to letting your children use your PC and get online safely.

Introducing Settings

This is all achieved in the Windows 11 Settings panel. You will see *Settings* pinned to the Start Menu and represented by a gear (cog) icon. Opening settings reveals the different settings categories, listed down the left side, and the settings appropriate to that category in the main view, see Figure 2-1.

© Mike Halsey 2022
M. Halsey, *Windows 11 Made Easy*, https://doi.org/10.1007/978-1-4842-8035-5_2

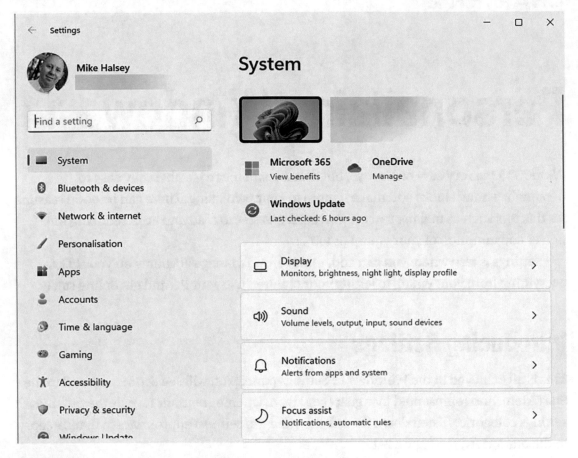

Figure 2-1. *Settings is available from the Start Menu*

It is here that you will perform every task from configuring and customizing your Windows installation to managing user accounts, work accounts, printers and Bluetooth headphones, privacy, accessibility, and more.

Personalizing Your Desktop

Let's start with your desktop and Start Menu. There are two ways to access the personalization options in Windows 11. You can either open *Settings* and click *Personalization* on the left of the settings panel, or you can right-click (tap and hold) anywhere in an unused place on the desktop and from the menu that appears click *Personalize.*

Windows 11 has personalization settings for all parts of the desktop and user experience. The first thing you will see is a selection of themes, which include different color schemes for Windows, and also different desktop wallpapers, see Figure 2-2.

Figure 2-2. Windows 11 comes with a selection of desktop themes

Some of these themes, such as the one seen in Figure 2-2, will change the whole desktop from a light theme to a dark one. Others will change the colors of specific desktop items such as the Taskbar and Start Menu.

Tip Dark themes, often called *Dark Mode*, can make your PC screen easier to read and help reduce eyestrain. If your laptop or PC has a screen with an OLED or an AMOLED display (refer to the device specifications to see if it has one of these display types), then dark mode can also help reduce power consumption, as if a pixel on the screen is black, it draws no power from the battery at all.

If you scroll down the Personalization options screen with your mouse or finger, you will see additional options, allowing you to change any aspect of the current theme, see Figure 2-3.

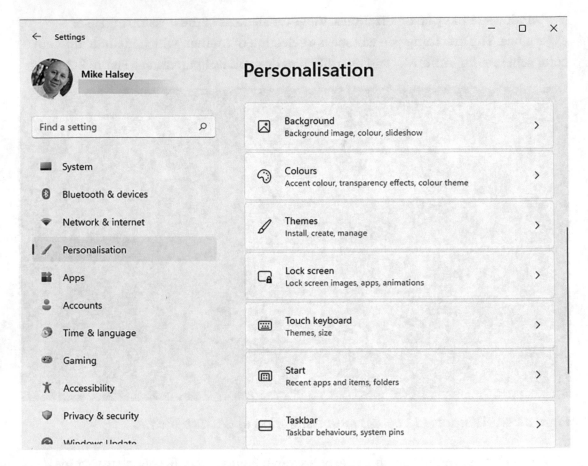

Figure 2-3. *You can personalize any aspect of a desktop theme*

The options available to you include the following:

- **Background** is where you can change the desktop background (often known as a wallpaper) between a picture, a solid color, or a slideshow of photos and choose your own photo from your file library as your desktop background.

- **Colors** lets you switch between light and dark modes, turn transparency effects off (which can make the desktop easier for some people to see), and change the accent color for your desktop (which will affect the Taskbar, Start Menu, and open apps, allowing you to personalize your desktop further).

- **Themes** is where you can further personalize the current desktop theme by changing Windows 11's sounds and the mouse cursor (we'll look at this more in Chapter 6). Additionally, you can get more desktop themes from Microsoft from these settings.

- **Lock Screen** allows you to choose a background picture, or a solid color for the Lock Screen, as well as choose if additional information such as the weather, and any new email or current calendar events are displayed.

- **Start** is where you can personalize the Start Menu by having it highlight your most often used apps and by hiding your recent files and documents from being displayed.

Tip   At the bottom of the *Start* options is a section called *Folders*. This allows you to pin additional quick link icons to the Start Menu for Windows features such as Settings, File Explorer, and your Personal Files folder. These will appear next to the power button at the bottom right of the Start Menu.

- **Taskbar** lets you turn on and off some of the icons that appear on the Start Menu, including the *Search* and *Task View* icons that we looked at in Chapter 1, and also the *Widgets* and *Chat* icons which we will look at in Chapters 3 and 7.

Tip   If you prefer the Start Button and Start Menu to appear on the left of the Taskbar as they did with earlier versions of Windows, you can select this option in the *Taskbar behaviors* options, along with turning notification badges off for the app icons on the Taskbar.

Changing Windows Desktop Scaling

One of the problems with modern computer displays is they come with a very high resolution. While this can make apps, games, photos, and videos look pin sharp, it can also make everyday items on the desktop such as text and icons very small and difficult to read.

In Settings, select *System* in the left panel, and then *Display* on the right side (you can also get to this by right-clicking the desktop and selecting *Display settings* from the menu that appears).

In the Display settings options, you will see an option called *Scale*. There is a drop-down menu here which has different scaling options for your display, and they will vary from 100% all the way to 250%, see Figure 2-4.

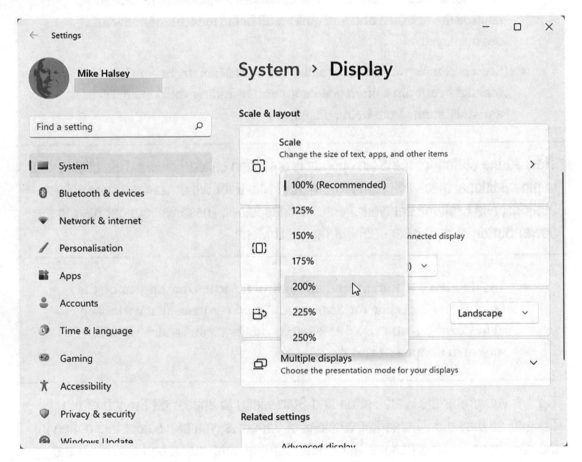

Figure 2-4. *You can change the size of text and icons using scaling*

Changing the scaling options doesn't change how pin sharp apps, games, photos, and video can look as they still stay the same. What it changes is the size of text and icons on your desktop, making them much easier to see and read (if you zoom upward) or to give you more available desktop space overall (if the zoom level goes downward).

Caution Changing your desktop scaling options is not the same thing as changing the *Display resolution*, as the latter will make your display blocky and difficult to use. Display resolution should always be set to the native resolution of your PC's monitor.

Personalizing Your Sound Options

Sometimes, especially when you've plugged a different monitor into your PC, you can find that your sound isn't working. This happens when Windows thinks you want to play your sound through a different device than the one you actually want. You can choose what device or speakers to play your sound on in Settings under *System* and *Sound*, see Figure 2-5.

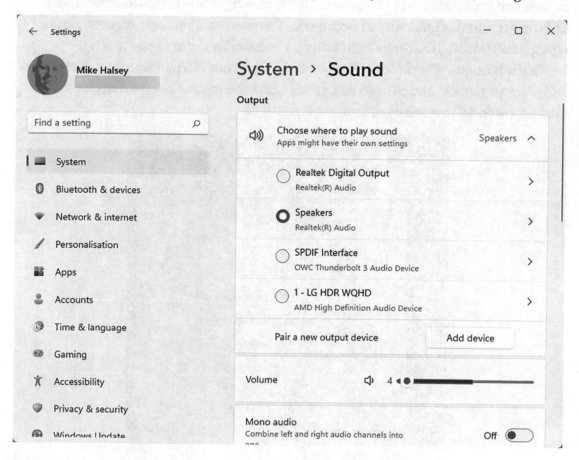

Figure 2-5. You can control sound and audio in Settings

In the section *Choose where to play sound*, you can select which audio device to use with your PC. This can come in useful if you plug headphones into your PC, perhaps for an online call or meeting, but they're not recognized.

You will see a volume slider below this where you can select the volume for your PC, and further down the page is also a *Choose a device for speaking and recording* panel, and you can use this to select the correct microphone to use for online calls and meetings.

Note that if you are using Bluetooth headphones or speakers and they are not visible in the list, I will show you how to connect and manage them in Chapter 10.

Personalizing Quick Settings

In Chapter 1, I detailed the Quick Settings panel, which pops out when you click the network and volume icons in the System Tray to the right side of the desktop Taskbar. This menu contains quick on/off switches for features like Bluetooth, flight mode (on laptops and tablets), the Night Light feature, Accessibility settings, and more.

In the bottom-right corner of the Quick Settings panel is a pen icon, and clicking this will allow you to add and remove items from Quick Settings, as well as dragging items around the panel to rearrange them, see Figure 2-6.

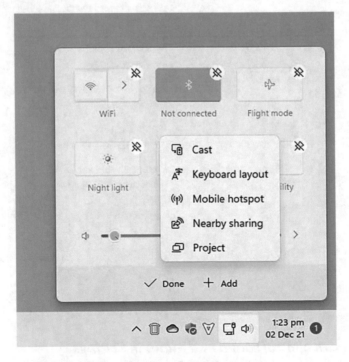

Figure 2-6. *You can personalize the Quick Settings menu*

You can click the unpin icon in the top-right corner of any item to remove it and also click the *Add* button to display a list of additional settings you can add. These will vary from one PC to another depending on the hardware and features you have installed. When you are finished customizing Quick Settings, click the *Done* button.

Adding and Managing User Accounts

You might not be the only person that wants to use your PC. Perhaps a friend or another member of your family wants to use the PC too, or maybe you want your children to be able to use it safely.

You can add user accounts to the PC in Settings by selecting *Accounts* from the left panel. The first thing it will show you is details of your own user account, see Figure 2-7, and below this are options to manage *Your info* which is where you can add or change your user avatar and add and manage *Email and accounts* which we will look at shortly, and to sign into your PC using facial or fingerprint recognition (called Windows Hello), and we will look at how we set this up and use it in Chapter 9.

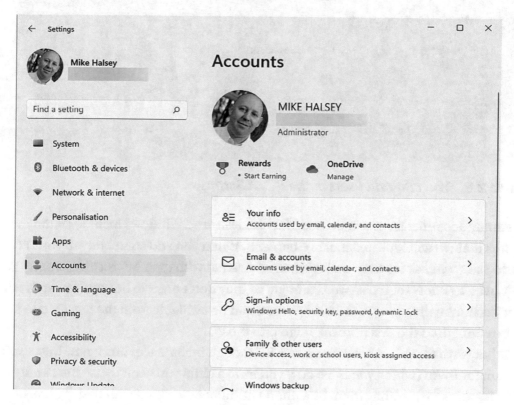

Figure 2-7. *You manage your and other user accounts in Settings*

You set up and manage other users on the PC using the *Family & other users'* settings. There are two different ways to add an account, *Add a family member* and *Add* [an] *other user*, see Figure 2-8.

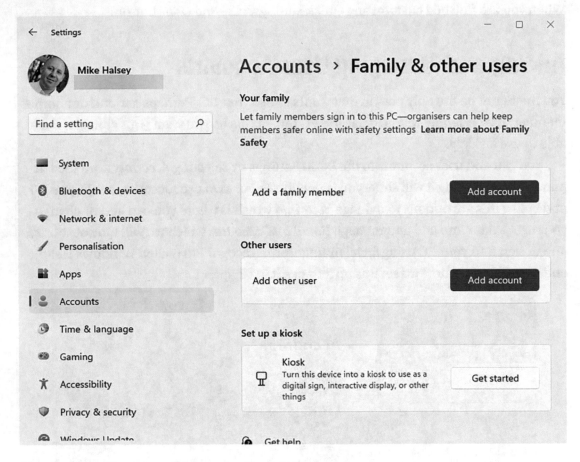

Figure 2-8. *You can add users to the PC in Settings*

Family accounts are normally used for children, and Windows includes family safety features that we will look in detail in Chapter 3. When you add somebody to your PC, Windows 11 will ask for the email address associated with their Microsoft Account. You don't need to know their password though, so they don't need to be with you at the time. Their account will appear at the Lock Screen and be available from the Start Menu and will be configured the first time they sign into the PC.

Other ways to add a user account to a PC though include creating a new Microsoft Account for them (which you must do if you have a child you want to use the Family Safety features for), adding them by a phone number associated with their Microsoft

Account, or if your PC is running Windows 10 Pro you will see an option to add a user *without* a Microsoft Account. This will just add a local (non-synced) account to the PC, see Figure 2-9.

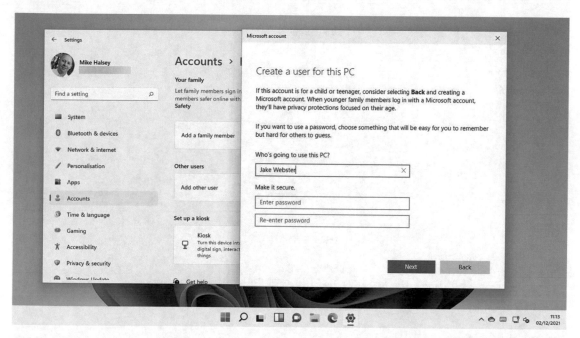

Figure 2-9. *There are different ways to add a user to your PC*

Note   If you really want to use local accounts on your PC but are using Windows 10 Home, you can upgrade in Settings by going to *System, About* and clicking *Product key and activation*. This will give you an upgrade option where you can purchase an in-place upgrade to Windows 10 Pro in the Microsoft Store.

After a user has been added to the PC, they will appear in the *Family & other users'* settings, and you can click their name to get more options. These include *removing* their account from the PC when it is no longer required and *Changing* [their] *account type*, see Figure 2-10.

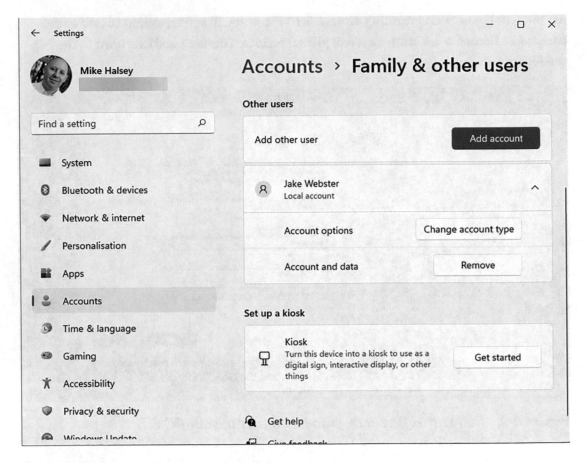

Figure 2-10. *You can change a user between two account types*

There are two account types available in Windows 11:

- **Standard user** can only make changes to the PC that don't affect other user accounts. They can install apps from the Microsoft Store but not ones downloaded from websites or installed from another disk like a USB flash drive. They also cannot add or manage users or change any settings on the PC except for their own personalization options.

- **Administrator** is a user like your own account that can change anything on the PC. People should only be administrators if you can trust they won't change things you don't want them to.

Managing Accounts for Children

I'm going to begin this section with a caveat. Microsoft do change the child account and family safety options in Windows and on their Family Safety website from time to time as they introduce new features or update existing ones. This means that what you see might vary slightly from what I detail here, though the functionality will always remain broadly the same.

When you add a *Family* account, you are first asked what *role* they should have. This is either an *Organizer*, and this is a role that would be assigned to another parent, guardian, or adult who is supervising the child, or a *Member* and this option is the one you would choose for a child, see Figure 2-11.

Figure 2-11. *You can choose from a parent of the child in the Family settings*

Once a child's account has been set up, when you are signed into Windows 11 using your own account, the child will be visible in the *Family & other users* settings, and you will see an option to *Manage family settings online...*, see Figure 2-12. This is where you can manage their safety settings.

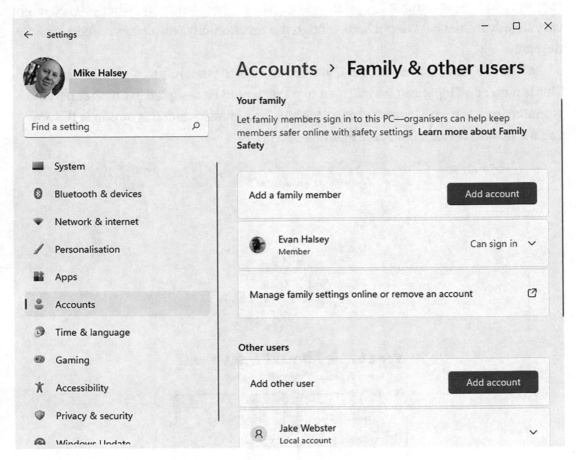

Figure 2-12. *You can access family options from the Settings panel*

Clicking this takes you to a website where you can see your child account(s), see Figure 2-13, and yes, I know this is showing a picture of my border collie Evan, but I don't have children of my own, and having some just for the purpose of writing this book might not be the best for them... or my own sanity.

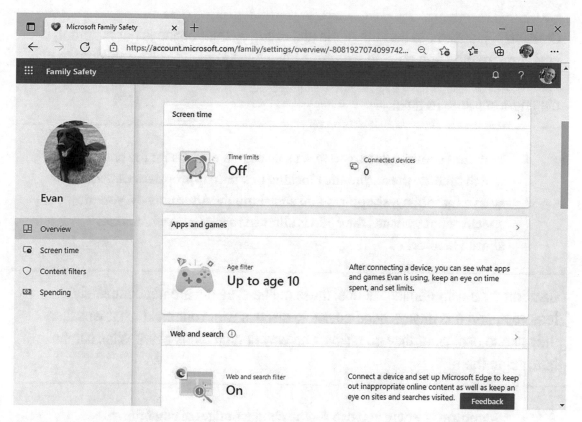

Figure 2-13. *You manage family safety features online*

This is a website you might want to bookmark; I'll show you how to do this in Chapter 3, as you'll want to come back to it regularly. While there's still a caveat with this as Microsoft might vary or retitle these options over time, the main options available to you include the following:

- **Screen time** is where you can manage the amount of time and times of the day when the child can use Windows 11 and other Microsoft devices such as an Xbox games console.

- **Apps and games** is where you can set an age rating for games; 10 in the case of Evan as he had his tenth birthday a few months ago. This works with online game age rating systems to help make sure your child does not play inappropriate games.

Caution   Please note that the game age rating system online is not foolproof, and some games and gaming platforms have been known to allow children to play age-inappropriate games. It is always advisable to check what games your child is playing from time to time.

- **Web and search** allows you to set safe search options for the child, which include the automatic blocking of age-inappropriate websites such as gambling, shopping, and social media. Alternatively, you can specify what websites the child is allowed to visit, and which ones should be blocked.

Caution   As with gaming ratings, these online systems are not completely foolproof, and it is always good advice to discuss with your child what websites they like to use, what they do online, and why certain types of websites can be harmful to them.

- **Spending** is where you can set the child a budget of what they are allowed to spend on apps and on in-app purchases (which have been known to bankrupt a few people when it all goes horribly wrong), or you can specify that you must give permission whenever your child wishes to make a purchase online.

- **Xbox online gaming** is an additional set of options that are part of the Xbox online gaming system, which allow you to help shield your child from inappropriate games and online spending.

Setting Up Email and Online Accounts

Windows 11 comes with in-built email and calendar apps, but you might use a non-Microsoft Account for these, such as an account from Google. Additionally, you might also use your PC for work and want access to your work email and calendar, and we will look at working on your PC in detail in Chapter 8.

In Settings, click *Accounts* and then *Email & accounts* to set up (and remove) additional accounts on your PC. When you click the *Add account* button, you will be asked what type of account you want to add; these include Microsoft and Microsoft 365 accounts and Google, Yahoo!, and Apple iCloud accounts, and there is an advanced setup option for other types of accounts, see Figure 2-14.

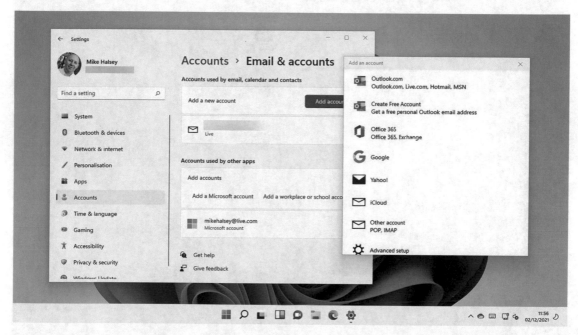

Figure 2-14. *You can add email and other accounts to your PC*

You can add as many accounts as you need and these will be available in appropriate apps, such as email and calendar.

The Email and Calendar Apps

You can find both the Email (called Mail in Windows 11) and Calendar apps in the Start Menu, and they are pinned to the Start Menu when you first start using Windows 11, see Figure 2-15. I am not going to spend much time on these apps; however, as Microsoft update them regularly and as I write this, I have already said a complete overhaul is coming to them, to bring them more in line with the look, feel, and functionality of their **Outlook.com** online email and calendaring website.

Figure 2-15. *You can find the email and calendar apps in the Start Menu*

Summary

It's very easy to work with multiple people on a PC, and when you have your own files, documents, settings, and saved games on the PC, it's a good idea for each person to have their own account too, or else they might change something in your account you would prefer they didn't. Microsoft do make this very easy to do, though remember you will need Windows 10 Pro to use a local account.

The very next thing you will want to do with your PC though is to get online and to start browsing the Internet. In the next chapter then we'll look at how you connect your PC to Wi-Fi and local networks, how to get started with Microsoft's Edge web browser, and how to set up your online experience to be safe and secure.

CHAPTER 3

Getting Online and Using the Internet

What's the use of a computer if you can't use it to get online? This question fascinates me as I began using computers in 1981, and full 18 years before I used the Internet for the first time, and I used them in various forms every day thereafter, from home computers like the Sinclair ZX Spectrum to Psion handheld PDAs (portable digital assistants), and my first PC, an Olivetti, that couldn't have connected to the Internet if I'd have wanted it to.

This might be the same for you, but we can reminisce about the "good old days" as time moves on, and today I'd be completely lost without being able to manage my shopping, household bills, banking, and even my job online. I live in France, my publisher is based in New York (USA), and some of the editorial staff are based in various other countries around the world including India. I very much doubt I'd be doing what I do today without the Internet.

Luckily, it's extremely easy and straightforward to get online these days, but you do need to be careful. The first computer virus I was infected by just played "Yankee Doodle Dandy" to me every day at five o'clock. These days you risk having your identity, your money, and your data and files stolen.

Not that this is a reason to stay offline, so in this chapter, we'll look at how you get online with Windows 11, but crucially how you do it safely and securely so that you can go about your everyday business without having to constantly worry.

© Mike Halsey 2022
M. Halsey, *Windows 11 Made Easy*, https://doi.org/10.1007/978-1-4842-8035-5_3

Connecting to Wi-Fi Networks

If you are using a desktop PC and are connected via an Ethernet cable, this will be plugged into both the PC and your Internet router, and the connection will just happen and be there. Most people these days though connect via a mobile device such as a laptop or tablet, and for this, we need Wi-Fi.[1]

The best and easiest way to connect to a Wi-Fi network is through the Quick Settings panel. Open this and one of the first things you will see is a Wi-Fi icon, see Figure 3-1.

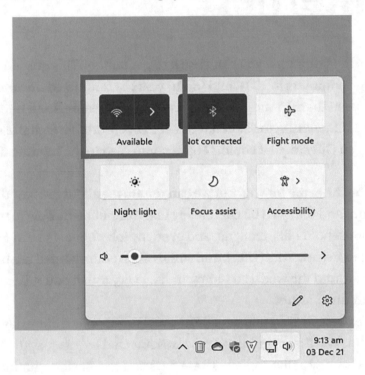

Figure 3-1. *You connect to a Wi-Fi network in the Quick Settings panel*

---

[1] One of the technologies that make both Wi-Fi and Bluetooth possible is called "spread spectrum technology," and it was invented in the 1940s by Hollywood starlet and leading lady Hedy Lamarr. She had starred in a host of blockbuster movies alongside Spencer Tracy, Clark Gable, and others but was also a genius inventor. Working with the US Navy, she invented the technology to help prevent Axis powers from jamming Allied torpedoes during the Second World War. The technology is still used in our computers and smartphones today, and she remains my greatest tech hero. If you find it on streaming, I highly recommend watching *Bombshell: The Hedy Lamarr Story* (Reframed Pictures, 2018).

There are two buttons here. The one on the left turns Wi-Fi on and off on your PC, while the arrow on the right will display a list of available networks that you can connect to, see Figure 3-2. Just click the name of the network you want to connect to, and you will be connected straightaway, or asked to enter the password for the network.

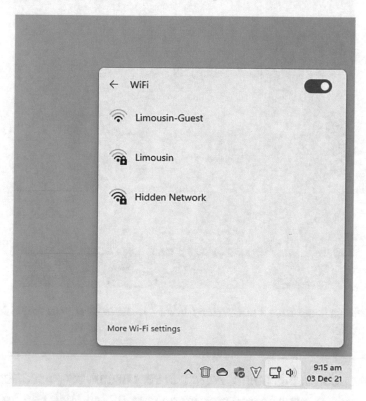

Figure 3-2. *Quick Settings displays a list of available Wi-Fi networks*

Sometimes you need more control over a Wi-Fi network, because perhaps it is being provided by a cellular data source such as a 5G modem. If you right-click on the name of the Wi-Fi network, some menu options will appear, see Figure 3-3.

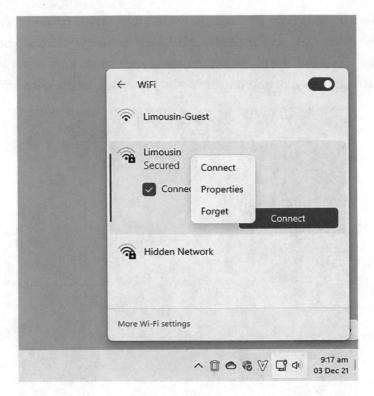

Figure 3-3. *You can get more control of Wi-Fi networks if you need to*

Tip   The last option in this menu, *Forget,* is very useful. Very occasionally, Wi-Fi network connections can become corrupt on your PC, and you can find yourself completely unable to connect. Should this happen, click *Forget* and the currently stored settings for the network will be deleted. When you reconnect to the network, it will be as though it were for the first time, so you will need the password if there is one.

Click *Properties* and additional options for that Wi-Fi network will appear in a Settings window, see Figure 3-4. Here you can set the network to be a *metered connection* if it is cellular. This will prevent Windows and your installed apps from using too much data, such as installing updates for Windows or any apps on your PC.

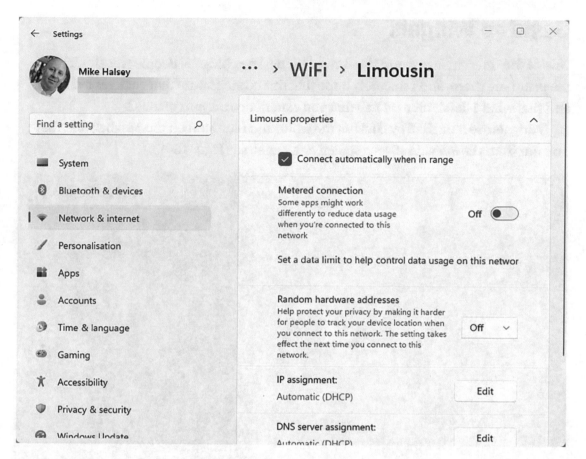

Figure 3-4. *You can manage data usage for cellular networks*

Caution   When you connect to an unsecured network, that is, one that does not require a password, or if you connect to a public network in a bar or café, you need to be sure to keep yourself safe as your laptop might be seen by other devices on the network. To achieve this, turn on the *Random hardware addresses* option in the network properties. You will need to disconnect and then reconnect to the network for this to take effect.

Desktop Widgets

One of the Internet features of Windows 11 is desktop widgets. People will either love these or hate them, and I sincerely hope that this is one feature that changes over time and that what I detail here *isn't* all that you experience on your own PC.

Widgets are launched by clicking the white and blue icon on the Taskbar, and they pop out from the left side of your screen as a panel, see Figure 3-5.

Figure 3-5. *Widgets fly out from the left side of your desktop screen*

Windows 11's widgets do much as you might expect them to and display information such as news headlines and weather forecasts, financial markets information, and your Microsoft To-Do list.

Clicking your avatar in the top-right corner of the widgets panel displays the widget options, including the ability to add and remove widgets from the feed, see Figure 3-6. In the bottom left of this panel, you will see a *Personalize your interests* option.

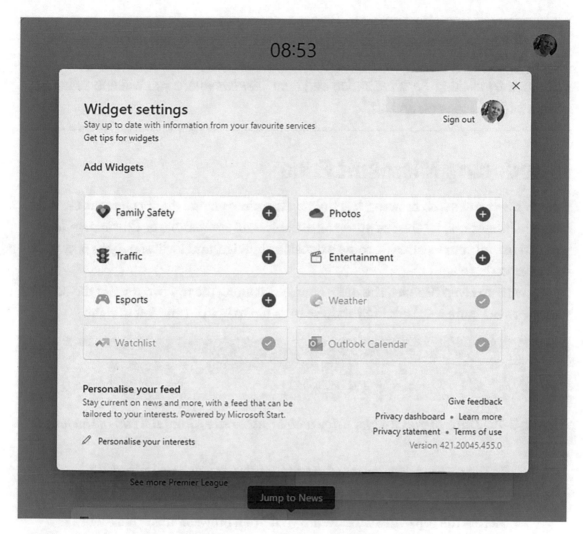

Figure 3-6. *You can add and remove widgets from Windows 11*

Widgets pull all their data from Microsoft's MSN news and information service and as I write this isn't especially useful. This is because there is an over-abundance of celebrity news, and third-party widgets are not currently supported.

I do expect this to change however, and hopefully by the time you read this, you will be able to plug in widgets from your workplace, more news and weather sources, and the websites on which you like to read stories and articles.

Tip   If you do not want to use Widgets in Windows 11, you can remove its icon from the Taskbar (as well as the *Search*, *Task View* and Teams *Chat* icons) in Settings by clicking *Personalization* and then *Taskbar* where you will see switches to turn these icons on and off.

Introducing Microsoft Edge

Edge is Microsoft's web browser; it is built on the same engine that powers the Google Chrome browser, so it is just as powerful, flexible, and compatible as Chrome. Indeed, you can use all your existing Chrome extensions in Edge, and I will show you how to do this later in this chapter.

As with any web browser, the main controls sit along the top two rows of the browser window, see Figure 3-7. Let's look at these from top to bottom and left to right.

Figure 3-7. *The controls for the Edge web browser are along the top of the window*

- In the very top-left corner of the window is a *tab actions* button. We will look at this shortly as it provides useful functionality.

- Across the top of the window are your open browser tabs. These will be titled with the web page they are displaying, and you can drag them left or right with your mouse to re-order them.

- To the right of the browser tab is a plus (+) button. Click this to open a new browser tab.

- On the second row, we start with the browser *page back* and *page forward* buttons.

- To the right of the page forward button is the *page refresh* button.

- The main part of the second row is taken up by the *search and address bar*. Type your Internet search or web page address here and press the *Enter* key.

- At the right side of the search and address bar is an *add favorite* button. You can click this to add the current web page to your favorites list, and I will detail more about this shortly.

- After the add favorite button is a button to open your Internet favorites list. Again, I will detail how to use this shortly.

- The next button is the one to view and manage your Internet *collections*. These can be very useful, especially for work, present shopping, or research.

- You will then see your user avatar; if you have signed into Windows 11 with a Microsoft Account, you can use this to sync your favorites, usernames, passwords, and more between browsers. I will show you how to do this shortly.

- Lastly are three horizontal dots which bring up the main menu options for Edge. Let's start here.

Note   Microsoft Edge, like all web browsers, is a constantly evolving product, and it is regularly updated by Microsoft. While the core functionality will always remain the same, some menu items and layout features may change from over time from what I detail here.

Configuring Microsoft Edge for Safety and Privacy

One of the first things you will want to do in Microsoft Edge is to set your safety and privacy controls so that you are not being spied on and having your activity tracked by the websites you visit. In Edge this is very straightforward. Click the *menu* icon in the top-right corner of the browser window and from the menu that appears click *Settings*.

Tip   If you can't find a setting in Edge at any time, the top left of the Settings page contains a search box you can type in.

This displays the main settings page for Edge, and it can be well worth your time spending some time to look around as here you can change everything from the standard search engine you want to use to accessibility settings that make the browser easier to use.

In the options on the left side of the browser window, click *Privacy, search, and services*, and you will see three main options under the title *Tracking prevention*. This controls what information is supplied by your web browser to all of the many, and there can be thousands of them on a typical PC, cookies (little trackers websites leave in your browser when you visit).

Setting tracking prevention to *Strict* is highly recommended, and this will help make sure your privacy is maintained online, see Figure 3-8.

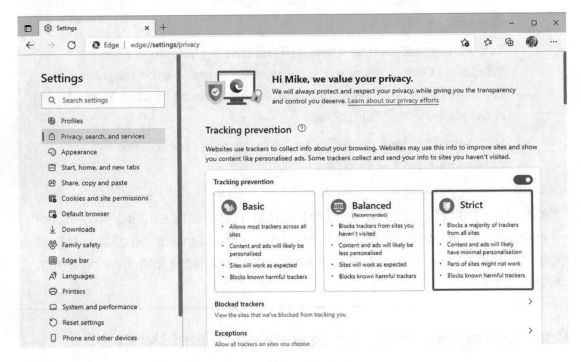

Figure 3-8. *You can block tracking cookies in Edge*

If you then scroll down the page, you will see a *Privacy* section. This contains a button called *Send "Do Not Track" requests*, see Figure 3-9. While this won't work with every website (as they don't all respect it), it will help prevent your activity being monitored and recorded by advertising and other companies.

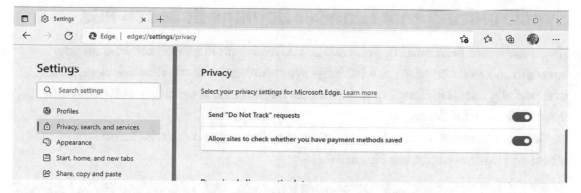

Figure 3-9. *You can request websites don't try and track you*

Further still down the page is an *Enhance your security on the web* section, see Figure 3-10. This is disabled by default as it can potentially cause problems with some (but very few) websites including banks and websites you use for work.

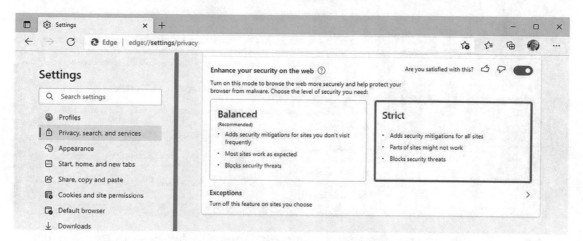

Figure 3-10. *You can enhance your security further online*

It is still worth turning this feature on and setting it to *Strict*. The reason being that if you find a website you need to use doesn't behave properly, you can return to this setting and click the *Exceptions* link to add that website to the list of websites exempted from this feature.

Synchronizing Your Browser Settings Between PCs

If you use more than one PC, or if you use the Microsoft Edge web browser on your smartphone, you can manage what Edge synchronizes between those devices. This is especially useful for keeping save Internet bookmarks, usernames, and passwords synced between different devices.

You can manage sync in *Settings* in the *Profiles* section, which is the first one you see when you open settings, see Figure 3-11.

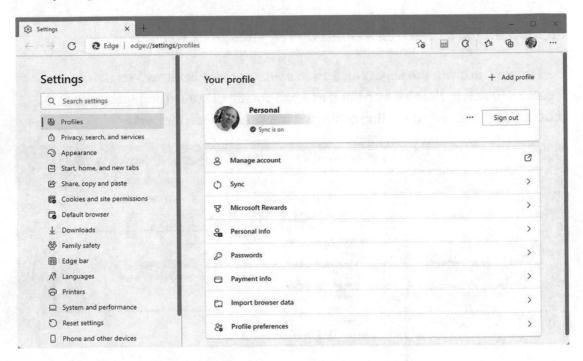

Figure 3-11. *You can synchronize settings and favorites between PCs*

Clicking the *Sync* option will bring up all the synchronization options available to you and allow you to turn sync on or off as you choose for that PC, see Figure 3-12.

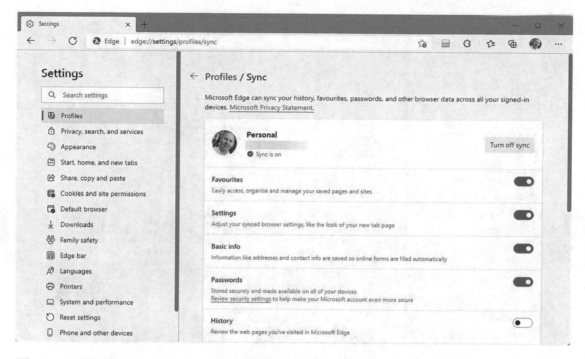

Figure 3-12. *You can choose what to sync between Edge browsers*

Tip   If you are switching to Microsoft Edge from another web browser such as Google Chrome or Mozilla Firefox, open *Settings* ➤ *Profiles* and click the *Import browser data* to bring your saved favorites, usernames, passwords, and more from that browser into Edge.

Personalizing How Edge Looks and Feels

The *Appearance* settings allow you to change how Edge looks and feels on your PC, see Figure 3-13. For example, you can choose from different color schemes, and if you scroll down this page, you can choose a *Page zoom* option, which can make the text and content on all new pages larger or smaller depending on your preferences.

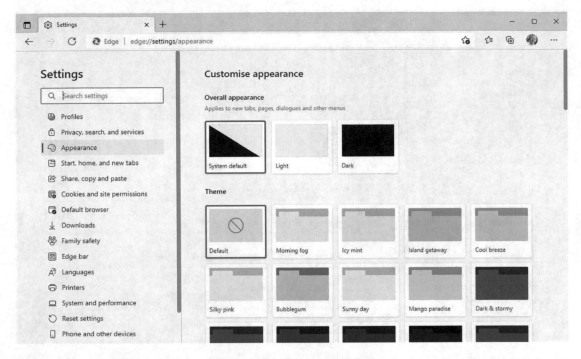

Figure 3-13. *You can choose how Edge looks and feels*

In the *Start, home, and new tabs* options in Edge's settings, you can choose what web page (or none) your browser starts with. You may want to reopen the page you were using the last time you closed the browser, or to start with a blank page, see Figure 3-14.

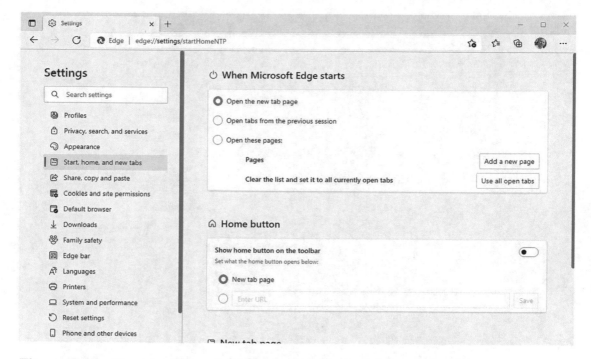

Figure 3-14. *You can choose what web page the browser opens with*

If you choose to use the Microsoft default web page when you open a new tab, this too can be customized. When you first start using Edge, it will show you the Bing photo of the day or some news headlines, but click the cog (gear) icon near the top right of the page and you can change every aspect of this page, see Figure 3-15.

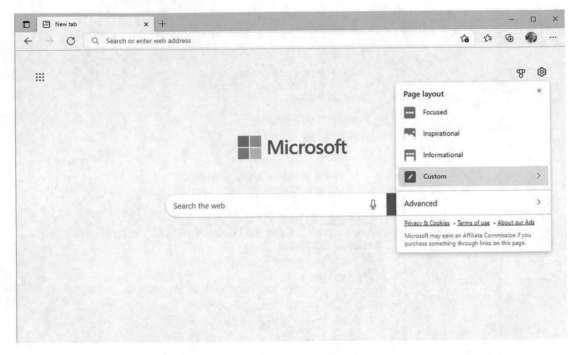

Figure 3-15. *You can customize the Microsoft default new tab page*

Working with Tabs and Web Pages

Earlier in this section, I mentioned there is a button in the very top left of the Edge browser window to help you manage your browser tabs. Click this with one or more browser tabs open and several options will appear, see Figure 3-16.

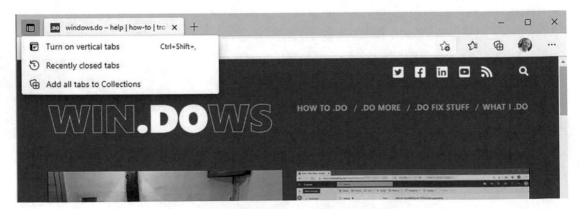

Figure 3-16. *You can turn on vertical tabs in Edge*

- **Turn on vertical tabs** allows you to have your tabs running down the left side of the page instead of across the top. This can be useful if you usually have a lot of browser tabs open and cannot read the titles of the web pages in those tabs.

- **Recently closed tabs** will display a history of the websites you have visited recently in Edge, useful if you need to go back to a website you were viewing earlier.

- **Add all tabs to collections** will create a new collection from your currently open tabs. I will talk more about collections shortly.

If you right-click on any open tab, you will see additional options, some of which can be extremely useful, see Figure 3-17.

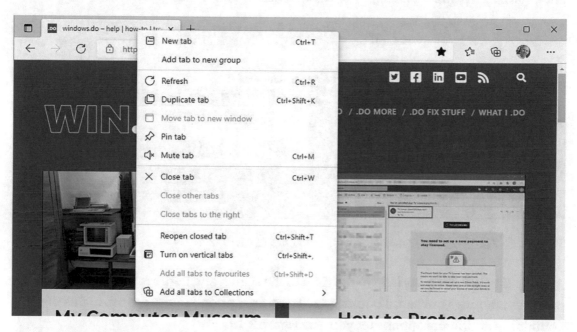

Figure 3-17. *Right-clicking a tab reveals more options*

- **Duplicate tab** will create a copy of the currently selected tab, useful if you want to have two copies of a tab open, perhaps to compare different options for something on that page.

- **Pin tab** will permanently pin the tab to your browser, so that it is always available to you. You can later unpin the tab in the same way.

- **Mute tab** is useful when a website is playing music or video and you would prefer it not to.

- **Reopen closed tab** will reopen the last closed tab, and if you then choose the option again, the tab closed before that one, and so on.

Using and Managing Favorite Bookmarks

You can save website bookmarks so that you can quickly return to them later. In Edge you do this by clicking the *Star* icon to the right of the search and address bar, see Figure 3-18. This displays options where you can change the name of the saved bookmark should you wish to and choose which bookmark folder (if you store your bookmarks in separate folders) to save the bookmark in.

Figure 3-18. *You can save Internet bookmarks in Edge*

Clicking the *Favorites* icon to the right of the search and address bar will display a menu containing your saved bookmarks. There are buttons across the top of this menu containing additional options for you, see Figure 3-19.

Figure 3-19. *You can manage all your bookmarks in Edge*

- **Add a new bookmark** allows you to manually type a web address to add it to your bookmarks.

- **Add a new folder** creates a sub-folder in your bookmarks that you can use to help keep them organized.

- **Search** lets you search through all your saved bookmarks.

- The three dots button displays additional options, including being able to *Open* [your] *favorites page*, here you can sort, arrange, and delete bookmarks.

- **Pin** will pin the favorites list to the right side of your browser window.

Using Collections in Edge

Collections are a different form of bookmark that are most useful when doing research or planning a project, such as a new purchase with different options, a house renovation, Christmas present hunting, or planning a vacation.

They help keep all your saved bookmarks together, but also allow you to add sticky notes or even just a part of a page, such as an image or photo. You open collections from the collection button just to the left of your avatar in the top right of the Edge browser window, see Figure 3-20.

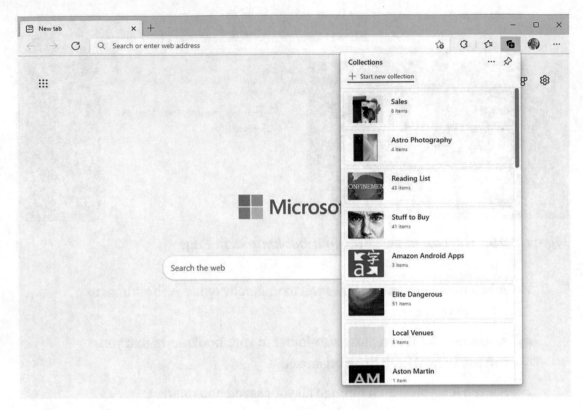

Figure 3-20. *Collections are useful when planning a project*

You can add a web page to a collection by clicking the collections button and then clicking the *Add current page* link. If you do not already have any collections in Edge, you will be prompted to create one. If you do have collections, open the collection you want to add the page to by clicking it and then add the page from there.

Tip   You can manage or delete a collection item by checking the box that appears in its top-right corner when you mouse over it, or by right-clicking it.

If you just want to add a specific image or a part of a web page to a collection however, such as some text, select it or right-click it with your mouse, and from the menu that appears, click *Add to collections*, see Figure 3-21.

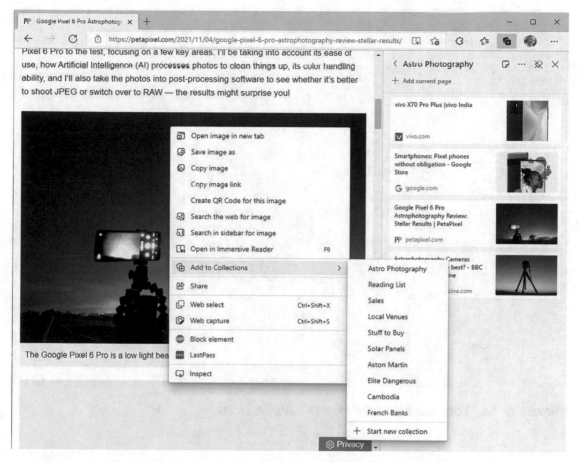

Figure 3-21. *You can add individual parts of a web page to a collection*

One of the ways that collections are far better than bookmarks when you are researching a project is that in addition to allowing you to add parts of a page, or individual images, you can also add sticky notes. With the collection open, click the *Sticky note* button to the right of the collection's name. This will display a sticky note that you write or draw on, see Figure 3-22. I will talk more about Sticky Notes in Windows in Chapter 7.

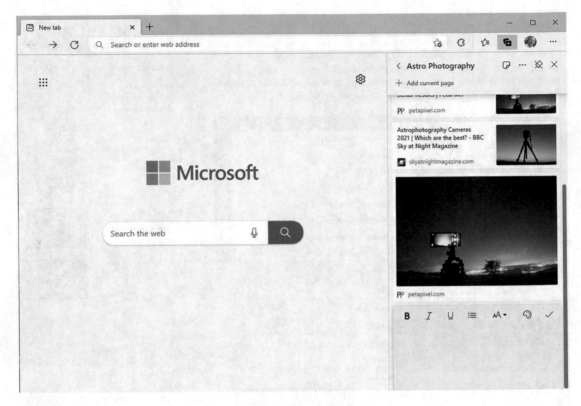

Figure 3-22. *You can add sticky notes to collections*

Installing and Using Browser Extensions in Edge

Just like other web browsers, Edge allows you to install and use extensions. You can add
extensions to Edge by opening the menu and selecting *Extensions*. This will take you to
the Microsoft Edge store, and you can search for and install extensions, see Figure 3-23.

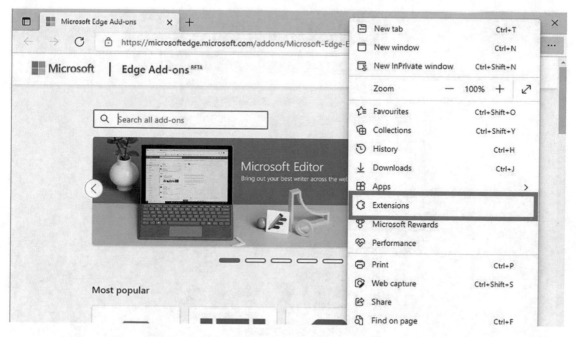

Figure 3-23. *You can install browser extensions in Edge*

Useful extensions to install can include advert blockers (I use Adblock Plus) and password managers like LastPass. When you click the *Extensions* menu option, you will see all of your installed extensions listed, along with a link allowing you to *Manage extensions*, see Figure 3-24.

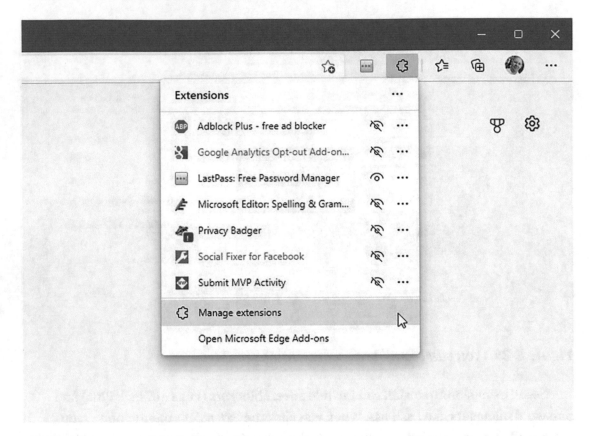

Figure 3-24. *You can manage your installed extensions in Edge*

Clicking this option takes you to a page where you can get details about, configure and remove your installed extensions, or just turn them off for a period of time, see Figure 3-25.

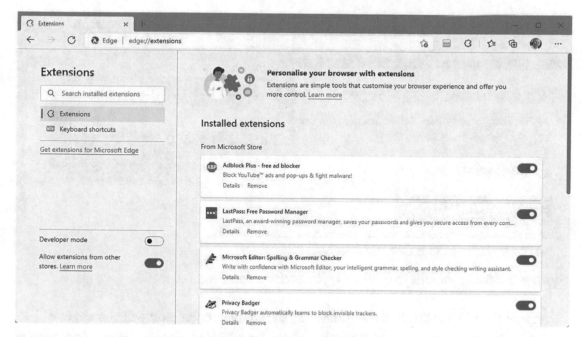

Figure 3-25. *Edge allows you to get detailed information about installed extensions*

Managing Internet Downloads in Edge

When you download a file from the Internet, you will see a small circular icon appear in the toolbar, and a small flyout tell you that the file is downloading, see Figure 3-26.

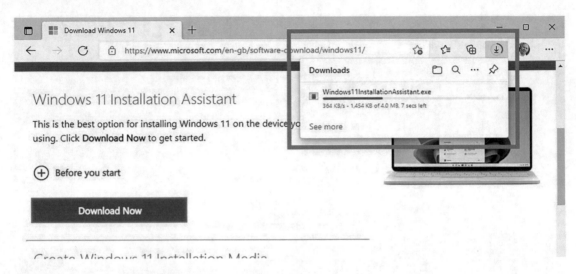

Figure 3-26. *Edge tells you when a file is downloading*

When the file has finished downloading, the small circular icon will change to a downward pointing arrow, and the name of the downloaded file will appear. At the top of this flyout menu are four additional options:

- **Open downloads folder** will open a File Explorer window where you will be able to see all of your downloaded files.

- **Search** downloads for a specific file.

- Get **more options** including taking you to a downloads page where you can view all of your downloaded files, and clear your download history.

- **Pin** the downloads menu to the right side of the Edge browser window.

You can also access download settings in the Edge Settings options. Click *Downloads* in the left panel, and you will be able to select the download location (folder) on your PC, see Figure 3-27, which by default is the folder labeled *Downloads* in File Explorer.

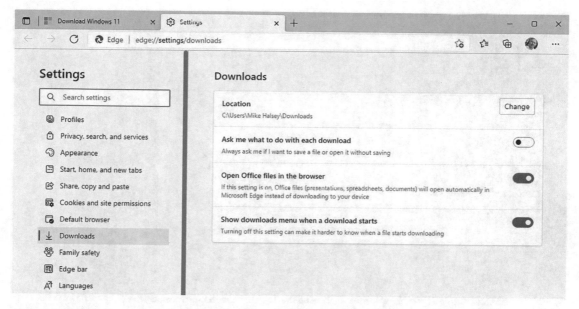

Figure 3-27. *You can choose where downloads are saved to on your PC*

Installing a Website As an App

If you use particular websites a lot, you can install them on your PC just so they look and behave like an app. With the website open in the Edge browser, open the menu, and select *Apps* ➤ *Install this site as an app*. This will then save an icon for that website to your Start Menu and open the app in its own window, see Figure 3-28. It can then later be uninstalled by right-clicking its icon.

Figure 3-28. *You can install any website as if it were an app on your PC*

Managing Shopping in Edge

Microsoft Edge has some shopping and coupon functionality built into the browser. Some people find this useful, especially the browser finding money-saving coupons for you, but other people can find the shopping functionality intrusive, especially as it can pop up entirely on its own without you needing to click on its icon.

You can manage this feature however quite easily. With the shopping or coupon pop-up displayed, click the three dots menu icon near its top-right corner, see Figure 3-29, and from the menu that appears, click *Disable shopping reminders*.

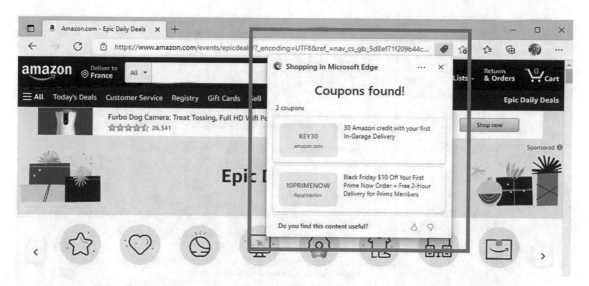

Figure 3-29. *It is possible to tame the aggressive shopping features in Edge*

If you search in Edge's settings for *shopping* though, additional options will appear, such as being able to turn the feature off altogether. Uncheck the *Save time and money with Shopping in Microsoft Edge* if you want to do this, see Figure 3-30.

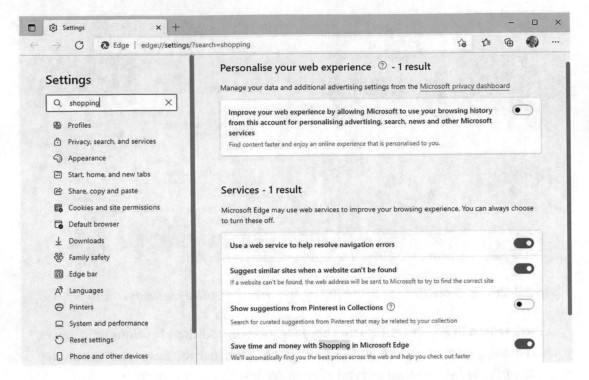

Figure 3-30. *You can turn off the shopping services in Edge*

Summary

Microsoft Edge is a hugely accomplished and fully featured web browser. As I mentioned earlier in this chapter, it is built on the same core engine as Google Chrome and as such is every bit as fast and compatible as Chrome and other competitors' browsers. For me though it is the privacy features that put Edge over the top, so it is well worth considering sticking with Edge.

The web browser might be the app you use most in Windows 11 though, but that doesn't mean you won't want to use other apps on your PC, and Windows 11 even allows you to install Android apps that you would normally only see on your smartphone. In the next chapter, we'll look at how you install, manage, and uninstall apps in Windows 11.

CHAPTER 4

Using Windows and Android Apps

When you think of installing apps, then there are probably two things that come to mind. The first is having to visit a website to download Windows software, being uncertain if it might be genuine or if it might have malware in it and installing it on your PC using an installer that dates all the way back to the early days of Windows. Indeed, many installers still ask if you want to add an icon to the Quick Launch bar which was retired with Windows XP in 2009.

The other way is to open the Apple iOS Store or the Google Play Store, doing a quick search for the app you want and then clicking one button to both download and install the app.

Microsoft know that the second way is best. It's more convenient, it's more secure, and it's just better all around. With Windows 11, they've taken this on board and not only expanded the number of ways in which you can get apps through the Microsoft Store, but they've also added the ability for you to download and install Android apps too.

Using the Microsoft Store

Before we get onto the headline act, let's have a look around the Microsoft Store and how you use it. You'll find it in the Start Menu, and it will be pinned there when you start using Windows 11, see Figure 4-1.

© Mike Halsey 2022
M. Halsey, *Windows 11 Made Easy*, https://doi.org/10.1007/978-1-4842-8035-5_4

Figure 4-1. *The Microsoft Store is pinned to the Start Menu*

When you open the store, you will find it's a fairly straightforward affair. Down the left side are category icons helping you quickly find *Apps*, *Games*, and *Movies and TV Shows* (note Microsoft have made noises about removing movies and TV from their library).

At the bottom of this panel is a *Library* icon that you can click to see all of the apps you have previously purchased or installed. This makes it very easy to reinstall them, or to install them on a different Windows 11 PC (and Windows 10 PC).

Note   Microsoft have expanded the range of apps available in the Microsoft Store with Windows 11, and you will now find many regular desktop (win32) apps there too, meaning you don't have to download them manually, and they will be updated automatically in the future.

At the top of the Microsoft Store window, you will see a search box that you can use to find apps and games, and your avatar icon, see Figure 4-2. You can click this display a menu of options such as managing your store payment methods, the different devices you have apps installed and activated on (as some apps limit the number of PCs you can run them on), redeem gift cards or codes, and to get further settings for app updating and privacy.

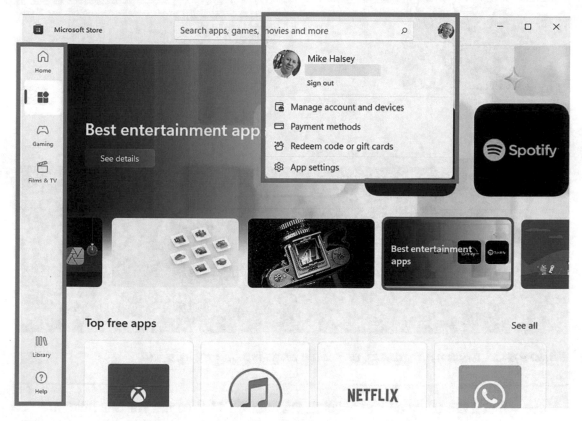

Figure 4-2. *The Microsoft Store is straightforward to navigate*

When you click an app, game, or video, you will see a button labeled either *Get*, if the item is free or if you have previously purchased it, or that displays the price of the item, see Figure 4-3. If you scroll down the page, you will also see screenshots, a text description, and any ratings that have been left by other people.

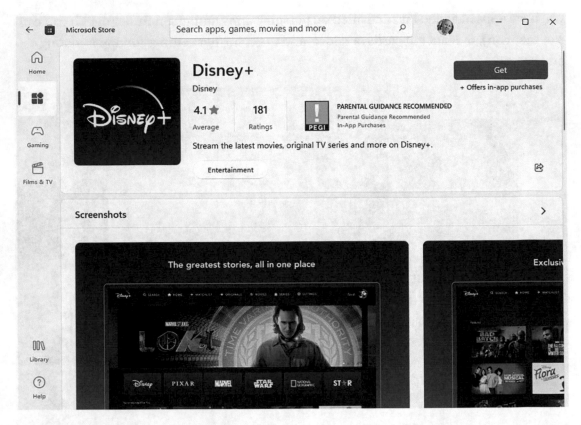

Figure 4-3. *Each app, games, or movie page is sensibly laid out*

Note   If you are using a local account in Windows 11 Pro, you will still have to sign into your Microsoft Account in the store to download apps and games.

Managing In-App Purchases

Many people, especially those with young children, can be worried about in-app purchases. These are purchases that can be made within apps and games, such as unlocking quick access to further levels.

Click your avatar icon at the top of the Microsoft Store and select *App settings* from the menu that appears. This will take you to a settings page for the store that includes an option titled *Purchase sign-in*. This should be disabled by default and that's how you want it, as you will then be asked to sign in with your password, pin, or with Windows Hello (we'll look at how you set this up in Chapter 9) to make purchases.

For children that are managed by Windows' Family Safety features, you can set a spending limit for them in the store and for the Xbox store that you can manage yourself. Check Chapter 2 for details of how this works.

Installing Xbox Games

When you buy Xbox console games, you will see that some are labeled as also being playable on PC, and you might also have purchased an Xbox Game Pass which allows access to a wide range of different free games each month. You can access these through the Xbox app which you can find in the Start Menu.

The Xbox app works in a similar way to the Microsoft Store, with category icons down the left side, and both a search box and your avatar picture, to access additional and account settings, at the top of the window, see Figure 4-4.

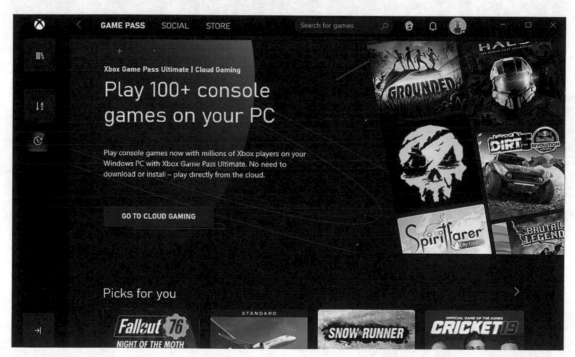

Figure 4-4. *The Xbox app allows you to install and play Xbox games on your PC*

Just as with the Microsoft Store, the Xbox app displays an *install* button when you click a game or will tell you how much the game costs to purchase. Helpfully, just below the name of the game, it also tells you how large the game download will be, which can help you determine if it's best left to download overnight, see Figure 4-5.

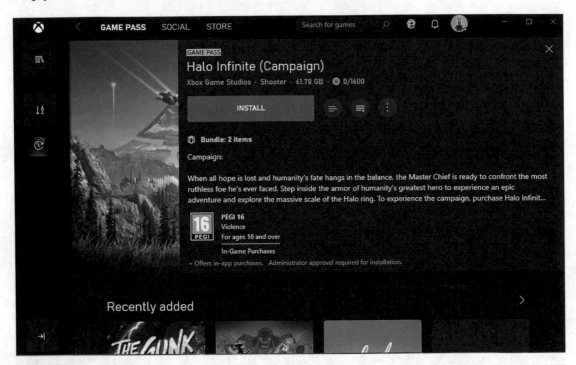

Figure 4-5. *You can install games directly from the Xbox app*

A Store Within a Store

One of the things Microsoft have added to Windows 11 is the concept of a store within a store, as third parties can now add their own store to Windows 11 and sell their apps and games through it. These third parties include the gaming library *Epic* and *Amazon* which we will come to later in this chapter.

If you search in the Microsoft Store for **store**, you will see available third-party stores listed in the search results. Clicking a store will allow you to download and install it on your PC, see Figure 4-6.

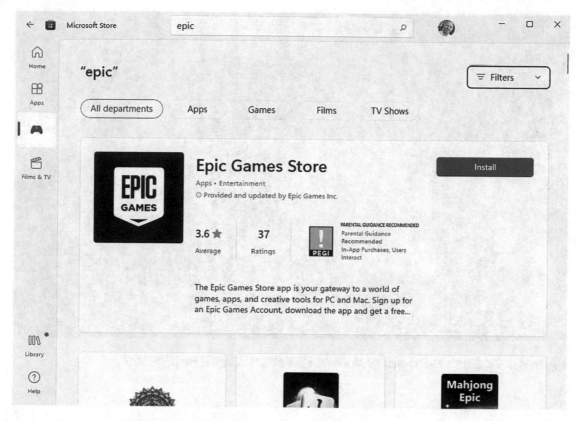

Figure 4-6. *The Microsoft Store allows you to download other stores*

When you have installed the third-party store, you will see it appear in the Start Menu, and you can open and use it from there. Each store will be different as each company has its own unique identity and way of working, but you will very likely already be used to using their own separate store app, or website to purchase apps and games, see Figure 4-7.

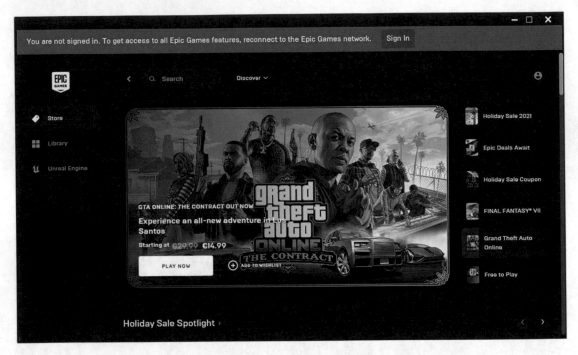

Figure 4-7. *Each third-party store in Windows 11 will be different*

Installing Android Apps on Your PC

Now we come to the headline act, being able to install Android apps on your PC. Sadly, this doesn't mean you have access to the full contents of the Google Play Store (though it is possible this may come at a later date) as Android apps are provided in Windows 11 from the *Amazon Appstore.*

Some Windows 11 PCs will come with the Amazon Appstore preinstalled, in which case you will see it pinned to your Start Menu, but everybody else can install it through the Microsoft Store, see Figure 4-8.

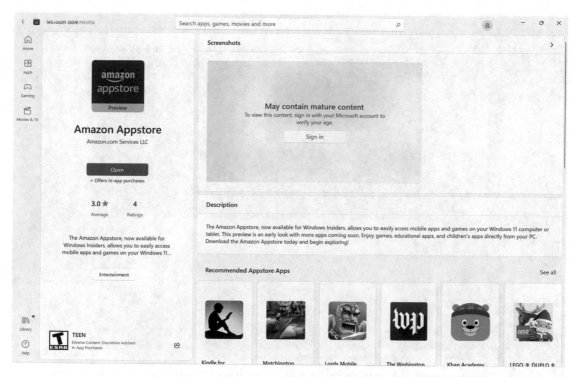

Figure 4-8. *The Amazon Appstore can be installed through the Microsoft Store*

While the Amazon Appstore doesn't carry the full range of apps and games in the Google Play Store, it does carry a wide selection including many of the most popular apps you use on a daily basis on your smartphone or tablet. Having the store now available in Windows 11 has also widened its appeal, with new apps being added to the Appstore every week.

Note   You will need an Amazon account to purchase and download Android apps from the Amazon Appstore, though the app allows you to create an account if you do not already have one.

When the Amazon Appstore is installed, it will appear in your Start Menu, and you can open it from there. It looks very similar to the Microsoft Store with categories for apps and games down the left side, and a search box at the top, see Figure 4-9.

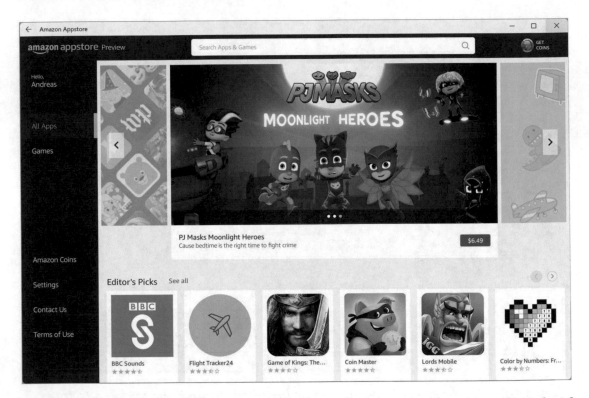

Figure 4-9. *The Amazon Appstore is where you can download and install Android apps in Windows 11*

Near the bottom-left corner of the Amazon Appstore is a *Settings* link. If you click this, you will see options for allowing in-app purchasing (note this is not controlled by Windows' Family Safety features), and to enable Parental Controls which you will need to configure separately, see Figure 4-10. From this screen, you can also set Android apps to be updated on your PC automatically.

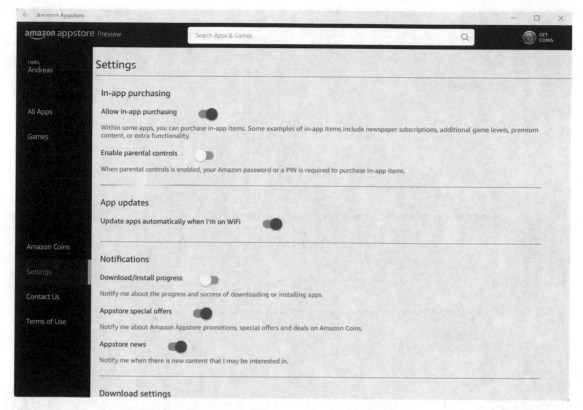

Figure 4-10. *You can change settings for the Amazon Appstore*

Uninstalling Apps from Your PC

Apps can be uninstalled from the Start Menu *All apps* list or directly from the main Start Menu if the app appears there or is pinned there. To uninstall an app from your PC, right-click (touch and hold) its icon, and a menu will appear with an *uninstall* option, see Figure 4-11.

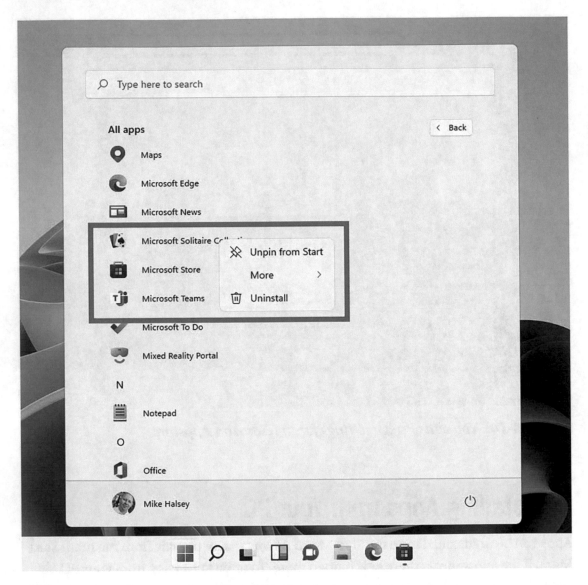

Figure 4-11. *You can uninstall apps from the Start Menu*

When you uninstall a traditional desktop app, it is likely you will be shown the older *Control Panel* interface where you must find the app, click it, and then click the *Uninstall/Change* button on the toolbar to remove the app from your PC, see Figure 4-12.

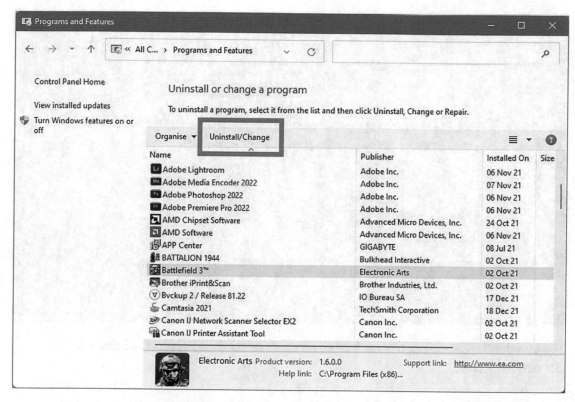

Figure 4-12. *Some traditional apps need to be uninstalled the old-fashioned way*

Introducing the Xbox Game Bar

If you are a keen gamer, and perhaps stream your gaming sessions to an online gaming social network, you will appreciate the Xbox Game Bar in Windows 11. Activated by pressing the *Windows key + G* at any time, it displays overlays you can use to capture and stream video, use voice, or text chat with friends and other gamers, monitor the performance of your PC, and capture screen grabs of important game moments, see Figure 4-13. You can activate the Xbox Game Bar at any time on your PC while gaming.

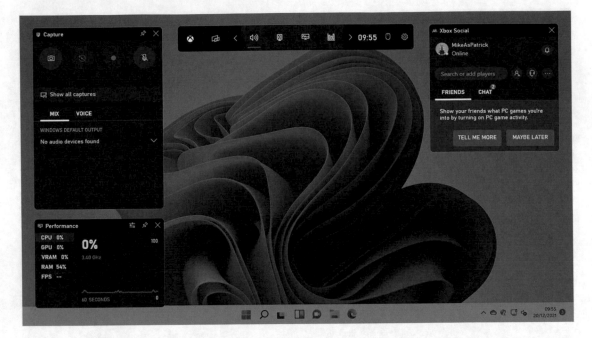

Figure 4-13. *The Xbox Game bar sits on top of your game and allows you to stream and chat*

Summary

Microsoft have made it really easy to install and uninstall apps from your PC; indeed, even many traditional desktop apps can now be uninstalled directly from the Start Menu without ever needing to see the older Control Panel interface.

The addition of Android apps and third-party stores only adds to the appeal of Windows 11. New stores are added on a semi-regular basis, so it's always worth revisiting the store from time to time and searching for **store** to see if there's anything new. Who knows, maybe the Google Play Store will someday come to Windows 11.

While we all like to enjoy ourselves, watch movies and TV, and maybe play games, the primary reason for having a Windows 11 PC is to "get stuff done," so in the next chapter, I'll show you how to manage, organize, and search for your files and documents on your PC and how to use Microsoft's OneDrive, cloud backup, and sync service.

CHAPTER 5

Managing Files, Documents, and OneDrive

We all have a library of files, documents, and photos. These are either letters and notes we have written for ourselves, reports and studies for work or college, or the huge volume of photos taken with our smartphone that we'll probably only look at once anyway. Storing these on our PCs is one thing, but making sense of them is something entirely different.

Maybe you're a neat freak like I am, with appropriately named folders, and subfolders, neatly organizing files, documents, pictures, and videos, or maybe you just have one huge Camera Roll folder with thousands of unorganized photos in it dating back more than a decade. However, you choose to organize, or not organize your files and documents, Windows 11 is on hand to help you make sense of it all.

Using File Explorer

In Chapter 1, I introduced File Explorer; this is the feature of Windows that lets you see, organize, and open your files and documents. Just knowing that File Explorer is there however is very different from being able to get the full benefit from it, so let's dive right in.

We've already looked at the toolbar that runs across the top of the File Explorer window. The options on this will change slightly depending on what you have selected, with some options grayed-out and inaccessible some of the time and others appearing only when necessary, such as an eject button if you click on a DVD or Blu-Ray drive.

© Mike Halsey 2022
M. Halsey, *Windows 11 Made Easy*, https://doi.org/10.1007/978-1-4842-8035-5_5

Working with Multiple Files

There are many occasions when you'll want to work with more than one file, as clearly working with them one at a time, to perform an action like copying or moving them, or deleting files, can be extremely slow and laborious. File Explorer offers you several ways to work with multiple files simultaneously:

- You can drag your mouse over multiple files, and you will see a colored selection box appear, see Figure 5-1. Any files that fall into that colored zone will be selected when you release your mouse button.

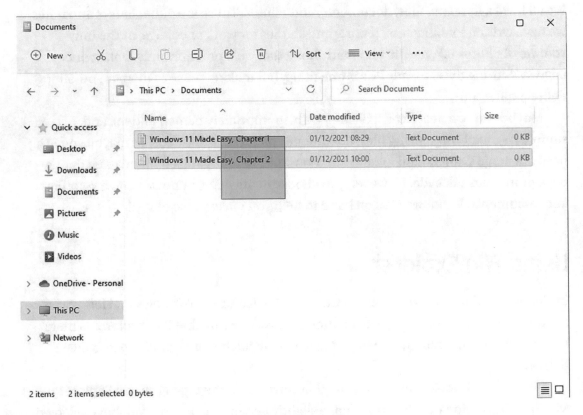

Figure 5-1. *You can select multiple files with your mouse*

- If you are using your keyboard, there are two ways to select multiple files. If you select files in a complete list, then click the file at the top (or bottom, it doesn't matter) of the list, and then hold down the *Shift* key on your keyboard when you click the file at the very bottom of the list; this will select all of the files between the two.

- Sometimes you want to select random files, or non-sequence files in a list. To achieve this, hold down the *Ctrl* key in the bottom-left corner of your keyboard when you click each file you want to select.

You then have different ways to work with your files. Across the toolbar, you have options to *cut* (move), *copy, paste, rename, share,* and *delete* files, but you can also move selected files by dragging them around the File Explorer window, perhaps into a subfolder.

Changing How Your Files Are Presented

Some people don't like their files to be presented in a flat list. This could be because you find the text for the files too small and difficult to read and the file icons themselves too small, or you want to be able to display more files in a single view.

File Explorer offers different ways to view your files, and this is done from the *View* menu at the top of the File Explorer window. This offers various options that include *Extra large and Large icons* (see Figure 5-2), Details, Tiles, and Content.

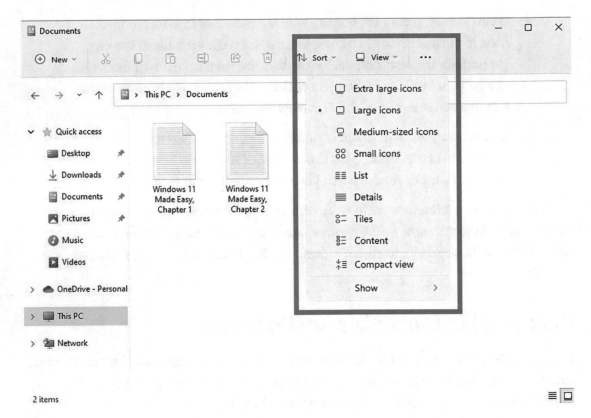

Figure 5-2. *You can present files in different ways in File Explorer*

If you have different types of files in a folder however, perhaps because you have a folder for a specific project, you can group files together in different ways. If you right-click in any blank space in File Explorer, a menu of options would appear including a *Group by* option. Hovering over this will display a submenu allowing you to group your files by *date* (which can be useful for your camera roll folder) and *type* and if you want the sort order to be ascending or descending, see Figure 5-3.

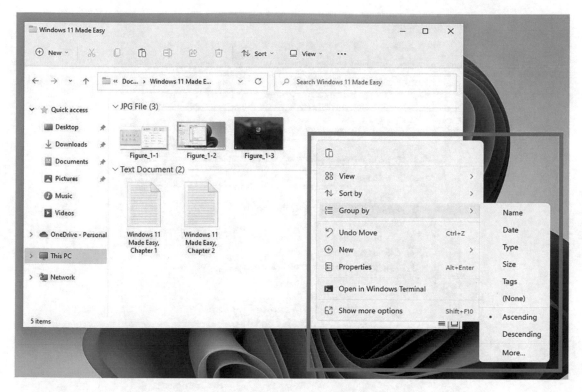

Figure 5-3. *Grouping files by type can help organize them*

It is definitely worth trying different views and grouping for your files and documents, as you will likely not want everything in every folder presented the same way.

If you want every folder to be displayed the same way, this can be done easily. Go to the folder at the top of the three, with all your other subfolders underneath it, such as selecting your *Documents* folder, and set its *View* and *Group* options to your preferences.

Next, click the three dots menu icon on the File Explorer toolbar, and from the menu that appears, click *Options*. A dialog window will appear in which you should click the *View* tab at the top. You can now click the *Apply to folders* button in the *Folder views* section, to make all the folders under this one look as you want them to, see Figure 5-4.

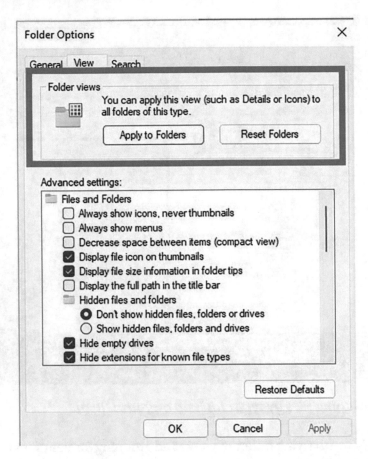

Figure 5-4. *You can make all folders on your PC display files the same way*

Creating New Files and Folders

Sometimes you need to create new files and folders, perhaps to create a subfolder to which you can move files for a specific school or work project to keep them organized, or photos so that you know they were all from a specific vacation or family gathering.

In Chapter 1, I showed you how to use the *New* button on the File Explorer toolbar to achieve this, but there is another option that you might prefer. Earlier on we right-clicked in a blank space in File Explorer to display additional options on how to display our files. This same menu also has a new option that allows you to create new files and folders, see Figure 5-5.

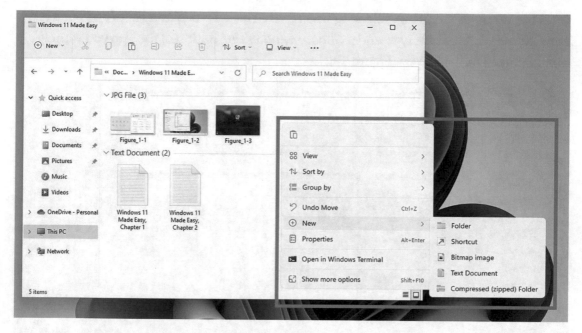

Figure 5-5. *You can create new files and folders from a right-click*

If you use this to create a new file or folder, the item will appear with its name ready for you to type whatever you wish to call it. This new item can then be dragged and dropped, cut, and pasted like any other item in File Explorer.

Tip   I will show you some great keyboard shortcuts to use in Chapter 12, but a quick way to use cut, copy, and paste in File Explorer is to use *Ctrl + X* (cut), *Ctrl + C* (copy), and *Ctrl + V* (paste).

Opening and Controlling Files

When you double-click (double tap) on a file or document in Windows 11, it will open in whatever app has been set as the default for that file type. What happens though if you have more than one app installed on your PC for handling files? Let's take the example that you might have a photo editor installed in addition to the *Photos* app that's part of Windows 11. You can open a file directly into a different app by right-clicking it and from the menu that appears selecting *Open with*. This will display a list of apps that are compatible with that file type and a *Choose another app* option, if the app you want is not displayed in the list, see Figure 5-6.

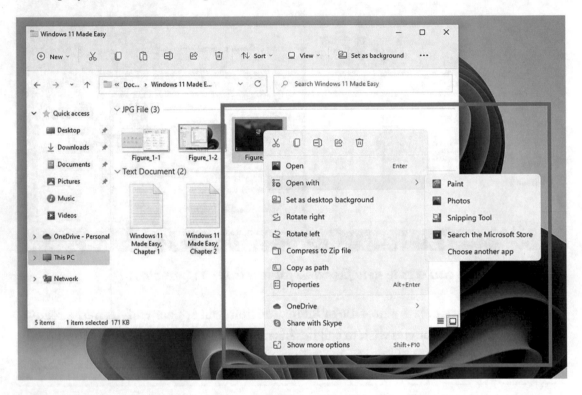

Figure 5-6. *You can open a file in a different app from its default*

You will also see that in this right-click menu, you can have additional options presented depending on what type of file you have selected. In this example, I have right-clicked an image, and options have appeared to *Set* it *as* my *desktop background*, and *Rotate* it *right* or *left*.

Searching for Files and Documents

We looked in Chapter 1 at how you can search for files and documents from the Start Menu, but File Explorer can give you more useful search options. Let's say, for example, that you want to find documents that were created within the last week, because these are the ones you are currently working on.

In the top right of the File Explorer window is a search box. Type in this for a search term (if you want to search for all files created by you, just type your name), and a *Search options* button will appear on the toolbar.

You can click this button to display options for narrowing down your search, see Figure 5-7. These include being able to search by the date the file was last modified or by the file type, such as a folder, note, or picture.

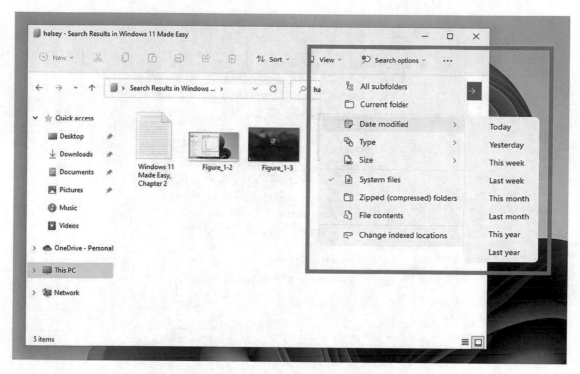

Figure 5-7. *Useful search options are available in File Explorer*

Personalizing File Explorer

You can personalize File Explorer in more ways. When you first open File Explorer, it will display the *Quick Access* view, which displays your user folders *Desktop*, *Downloads*, *Documents*, *Pictures*, *Music*, and *Video*, below which is a list of recently accessed files and documents.

To the right of this however is a link called *This PC*. Clicking this will change the view to display your user folders along with all the hard disks or removable drives (such as USB flash drives) connected to your PC.

If you want File Explorer to always display this view, or the Quick Access view to not display your recent documents, you can customize things. From the File Explorer toolbar, click the three dots icon to display a menu, and then click *Options*. A new dialog window will appear in which you will see various useful options presented, see Figure 5-8.

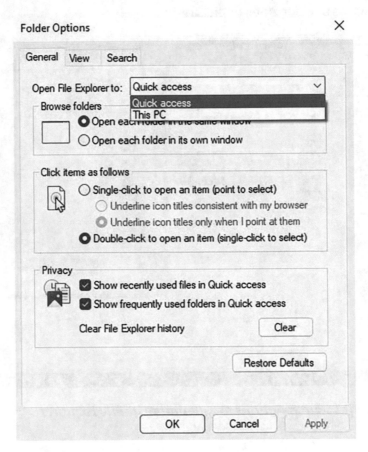

Figure 5-8. *You can further personalize File Explorer*

At the top of this dialog is a drop-down menu to choose if you want File Explorer to open with the Quick Access view or the This PC view. There is also a *Privacy* section in which you can ask File Explorer to not show your recently opened files and folders, or you can temporarily *Clear* the stored list.

Connecting to PCs and Storage on Your Network

You might have network storage, on other PCs, or on a USB hard disk plugged into your Internet router that has files or backups on it you need to access from time to time. You can access these by clicking *Network* in the bottom-left corner of the File Explorer window.

File Explorer will then present a message tell you that *Network discovery is turned off...*, see Figure 5-9. This is a security feature in Windows that hides all network devices automatically, but you can click the message to activate the feature and view your network drives.

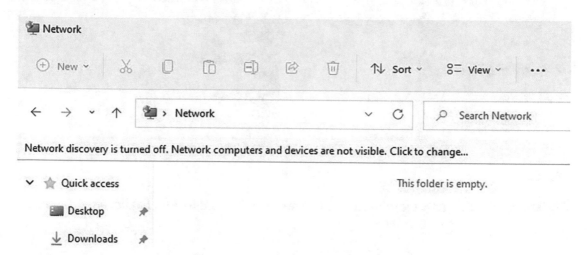

Figure 5-9. *You need to turn on network discovery to view and access remote storage*

With network discovery activated on your PC, the File Explorer view will change to show all available network storage and shares available to you, see Figure 5-10.

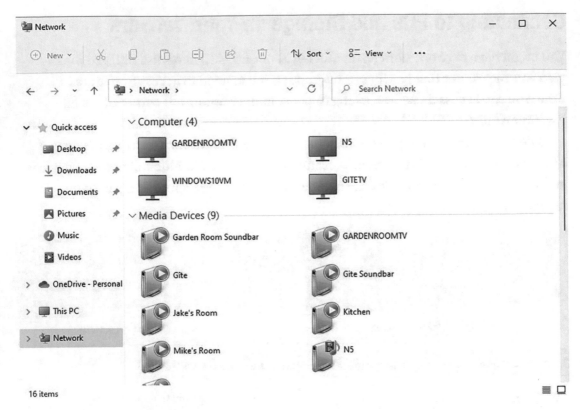

Figure 5-10. *You can view network shares and storage in File Explorer*

Follow the Breadcrumbs

Just underneath the toolbar in File Explorer is a useful feature canned the *Breadcrumb bar*. This displays your current position within the disk and folder structure on your PC (i.e., Documents) but can also do much more. If you are more than one folder deep on a disk, you will see small arrows appear between the different disks and folders. You can click these arrows to provide drop-down menus with quick links to other related places to go in File Explorer, see Figure 5-11.

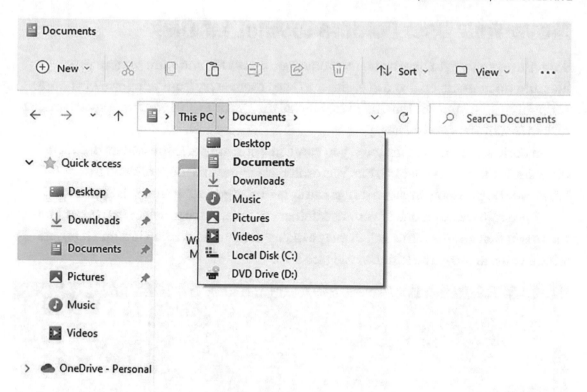

Figure 5-11. *The breadcrumb bar can help you get around quickly in File Explorer*

Additionally, you might sometimes need to know the exact folder location on the disk, perhaps because you are performing a task such as programming an app. To get this, click the icon to the very left of the breadcrumb bar, and the view will change to show you the exact technical disk and folder name you are currently viewing, see Figure 5-12.

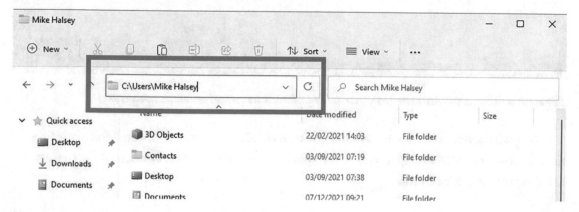

Figure 5-12. *You can view the technical disk and folder name if you need to*

Move Your User Folders to Another Disk

Sometimes you might have more than one disk in your PC and want to store your files and documents on that drive, either to keep them away from Windows 11 should something go wrong, and you need to reinstall the OS, or to give you more space on that disk to install apps and games.

In earlier versions of Windows, you could just cut and paste the folders between different locations on your PC, but Microsoft have made this more difficult in Windows 11, probably because things can sometimes go wrong with this approach.

If you *right-click* on one of your user folders though, you can select *Properties* from the menu that appears. This will display a dialog that has a *Location* tab, and it is here where you can move the folder, see Figure 5-13.

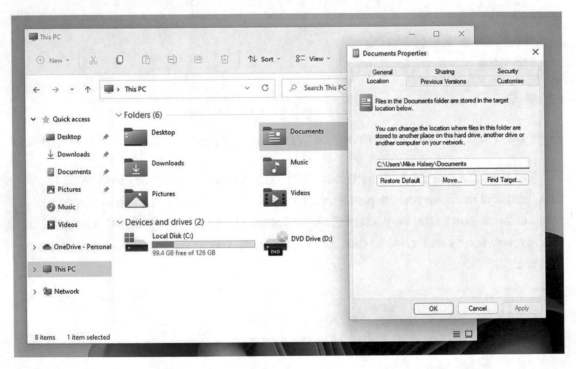

Figure 5-13. *You can move your user folders to another disk on your PC*

You will need to do this for each of your user folders, but it can help keep your files and documents safe and give you more space to install the latest version of Battlefield or Microsoft Flight Simulator.

Setting Up OneDrive on Your PC

OneDrive is Microsoft's file backup and sync service, and it's built into Windows 11. It can save and synchronize both your personal and work documents and is very easy to set up and use. You find OneDrive either by clicking *OneDrive* in File Explorer or by clicking the small cloud icon in the bottom right of the desktop Taskbar.

You will first be asked to set up OneDrive by signing into either your personal Microsoft Account or the Azure AD account provided to you by your workplace or school.

You will then be asked where you want to store your OneDrive files on your PC. By default, this will always be the drive on which Windows 11 is installed, in the *\Users* folder, but if you store your files and documents on another disk, as we looked at a little while ago, you might want to select a different location. Click the *Change location* link to achieve this, see Figure 5-14.

Figure 5-14. *You can choose a location to store your OneDrive files*

Once OneDrive is configured on your PC, you can control it by clicking its cloud icon, which you will find in the System tray in the right side of the desktop Taskbar. This will pop up a dialog in which there is a *Help & settings* button. Click this button for more options, and you will see a *Settings* link in the menu that appears, see Figure 5-15.

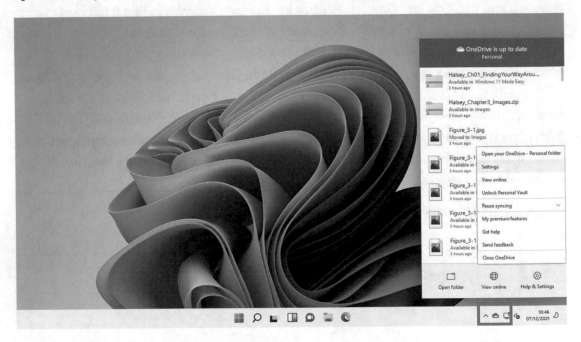

Figure 5-15. *You can configure OneDrive when it is running on your PC*

Configuring OneDrive

There are a few settings in OneDrive you might want to know about, as they can be very useful. By default, unless you already have files on your PC, OneDrive will display them as available on your PC, but will actually be leaving them all stored in the cloud and only download them as and when you need them.

Note   If you do want your files stored locally on the PC but like the idea of Windows downloading them as you need them, bear in mind that if you do not open a file for a period of 30 days, OneDrive will remove the local copy of that file to save space.

You might want all of your files stored on your PC all the time though, so in the *Settings* panel of the OneDrive options, you can uncheck the option to *Save space and download files as you use them*, see Figure 5-16. This will force OneDrive to keep all of your synced files on your PC.

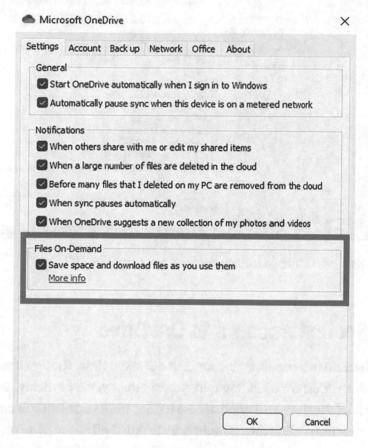

Figure 5-16. *You can force OneDrive to store all your files on your PC*

Additionally, you might want some, but not all, of your files in OneDrive to sync to the PC. You might be on a laptop you use for travel and want your documents and pictures stored there, but not your music and video. Under the *Account* tab in OneDrive settings, you will see a *Choose folders* button. Click this, and you will be able to uncheck any folders that you do not want synced to the PC, or check others that might not automatically be selected, see Figure 5-17.

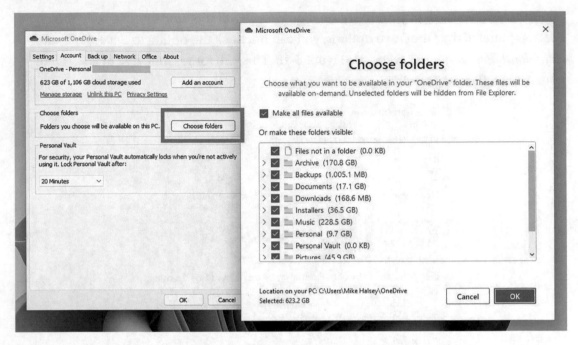

Figure 5-17. *You can choose which folders sync to your PC*

Adding a Second Account to OneDrive

OneDrive can handle two separate accounts at the same time, though it will not store the files in the same location as that would get very messy, very quickly. You might work from home some of the time and need access to files from your workplace.

In OneDrive settings, click the *Account* tab and you will see an *Add an account* button. You can click this to add either a personal or a work account, see Figure 5-18. Note though that you can have one personal account and one work account, but not two of one type.

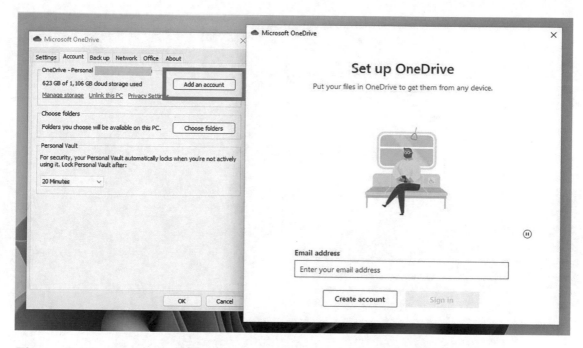

Figure 5-18. *You can add both personal and work accounts to OneDrive*

Summary

Windows 11 gives you a great many ways to organize, view, and manage your files on your PC, and even see them all the time when they're really stored in the cloud to save space on your PC or laptop. Searching is also intuitive and offers many features that can make it super quick and easy to find the files you are looking for.

In the next chapter, we'll build on what we've covered in this book so far and look at how we can make everything in Windows 11 easier to use, see, hear, and touch for everybody from those with poor eyesight and color-blindness to those with shaky hands or working in a noisy environment, and people with greater challenges when it comes to PC use.

CHAPTER 6

Making Windows 11 Easier to Use

Do you use a smartwatch? These handy (if you'll excuse the pun) devices are very popular, especially as fitness trackers. They're also useful for people who like or need to get notifications while at work, but who aren't permitted to use a smartphone, such as public-facing workers. I don't use a smartwatch though as, while I'm in perfectly good health, and not that old, my eyesight is just not good enough to let me read anything on a screen that small.

It's the same case with my laptop, where I would dearly love to use the screen at its maximum resolution, as I love having a lot of desktop space to work in, but I have to scale up that display otherwise everything is too small for me to see and read.

I'm just one example of someone who you wouldn't normally think of as needing or being able to benefit from the various accessibility settings in Windows 11. You don't need to have a special cognitive, motor, visual, or auditory need to be able to benefit. In this chapter, I'll show you how everybody from grandparents with shaky hands to people with color-blindness can benefit and have a better experience using their PC.

Make Windows 11 Easier to Use

Accessibility in Windows 11 starts with the Lock Screen. This is where you type your password or pin to unlock your PC and get to the desktop. However, here we could already hit a problem, both as the input box for your password can be quite small and also because the nice picture Microsoft like to place on the Lock Screen could make it difficult for some people to see.

© Mike Halsey 2022
M. Halsey, *Windows 11 Made Easy*, https://doi.org/10.1007/978-1-4842-8035-5_6

Tip   If you find it difficult using a mouse or trackpad to select a button or input box on your screen, press the Tab key on your keyboard to cycle between them.

In the bottom-right corner of the Lock Screen are several buttons. In the very bottom-right corner is a power button. Click or touch this and a menu will appear including Shutdown, Restart, and Sleep. Just to the left of this button is an Accessibility button. When you click or touch this, a menu appears with various options to help you use the Lock Screen, see Figure 6-1.

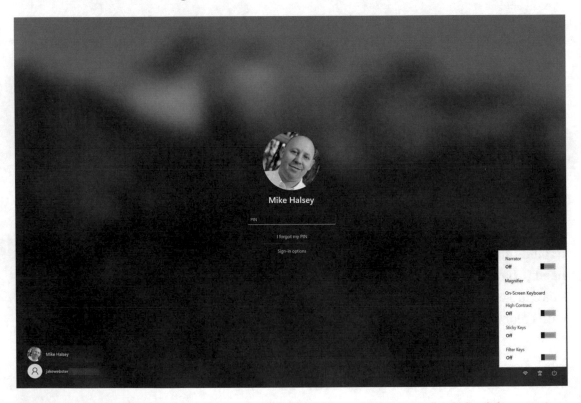

Figure 6-1. *Accessibility options can be found on a button to the left of the power button, in the bottom right corner of the Lock Screen*

There are four buttons. At the top is a switch to turn on the narrator, which will read what is on your screen through your PC's speakers. Next is the high-contrast mode which can make everything easier to see. Sticky keys below that allows you to perform actions such as Ctrl + a key or Shift + a key with only having to press one of them at a time, and Filter Keys changes the sensitivity of the keyboard so that the PC ignores repeated key-presses if you might hold a key down for too long. We will look at all these options in more detail later in this chapter.

Finding Windows 11's Accessibility Settings

There are two ways to find the Accessibility options in Windows 11. If you open the Quick Settings menu from the bottom right of the desktop Taskbar, you will see an Accessibility button, see Figure 6-2.

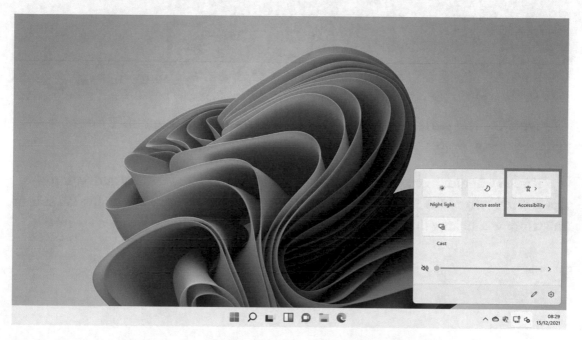

Figure 6-2. *The Quick Settings menu contains an Accessibility button*

Clicking or touching this button will display a menu of accessibility features that you can activate with a single click or tap. These options, from top to bottom, are the desktop Magnifier, Color filters, Narrator, Mono audio, and Sticky keys, see Figure 6-3. Don't worry for now if you're not sure what these are as we will look at then in more detail throughout this chapter.

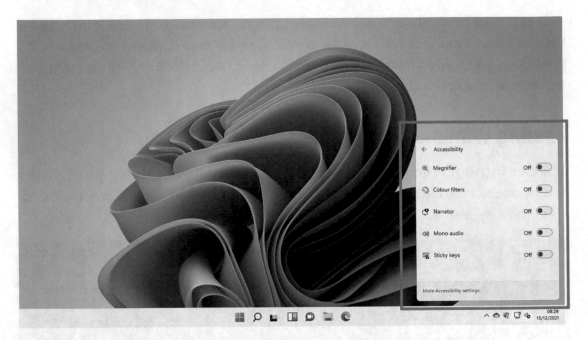

Figure 6-3. *You can activate Accessibility features with a single click from the Quick Settings menu*

If you want quick access to all of Windows 11's Accessibility settings and features, open *Settings* from the Start Menu, and you will see an *Accessibility* link on the left side of the window. Clicking this will display all of the options available to you, see Figure 6-4.

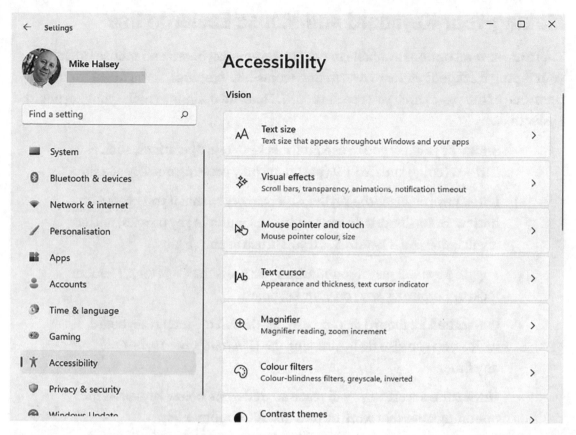

Figure 6-4. *Accessibility can be found as the ninth option down in the left panel of Settings*

Note   I want to add a caveat to the information in this chapter that as Windows 11 evolves and changes, some of this information might change too. The core functionality will always remain, but some of the options in Settings might change, and some new functionality may be added at a later date.

Making Your Keyboard and Mouse Easier to Use

There are several options available to help make your keyboard and mouse (including your laptop trackpad) easier to use. In the Accessibility settings, scroll down (or the right side of the page) until you see *Keyboard*. Here are options to make your keyboard easier to use:

- **Sticky keys** allow you to use multiple key press operations, such as Ctrl + C (copy) and Ctrl + V (paste), by only pressing one key at a time.

- **Filter keys** changes the keyboard sensitivity so that if you press a button for too long, it doesn't register as multiple key presses, and so it will ignore brief keystrokes if you brush against a key.

- **Toggle keys** will play a sound when you press the Caps lock, Number lock, or Scroll lock keys on your keyboard.

- **On-screen keyboard** lets you turn on the full on-screen keyboard, which you can also do by pressing the *Windows key + Ctrl + O* at any time.

- **Underline access keys** will place an underline below keys used for operating apps that work by pressing Alt + another key.

Also in the Accessibility settings are options called *Mouse pointer and touch*. Here you will see different mouse pointer styles, including high-contrast options, and a *Size* slider that you can use to make your mouse pointer larger, see Figure 6-5.

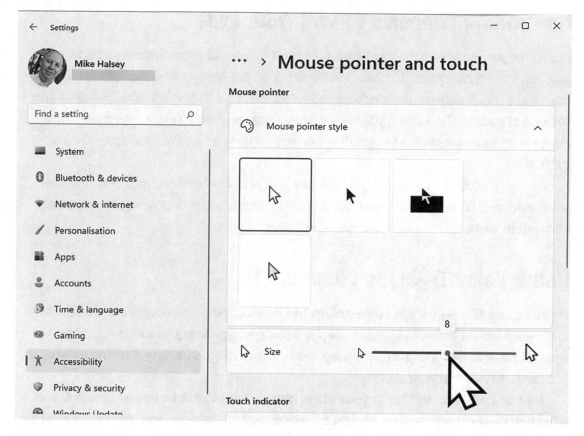

Figure 6-5. *You can make your mouse pointer larger in Windows 11*

Scroll down the page in the Mouse pointer and touch accessibility settings and there are more options available to you:

- **Touch indicator** will display a circle on the screen where you touch it using your finger, and there is a check box below this to make the circle larger and easier to see.

- **Mouse** switches to the general mouse settings. Here you can change your mouse from being right- to left-handed, change the speed at which the pointer moves on your screen, and change how the scroll works on your mouse.

- **Text cursor** lets you change how the text input cursor looks on your screen. You can activate a high-contrast text input indicator and change the size and thickness of the text input indicator.

Controlling Windows 11 with Your Eyes

For those people who either find it very difficult to use a keyboard and mouse, or who just can't use a computer that way, Windows 11 includes support for eye trackers. These are USB hardware devices that can sit on top of your monitor and that allow you to control your PC by moving your head or moving your eyes. They are perhaps most commonly associated with PC gaming, where people use them to look around on a battlefield.

In the Accessibility Settings, you will see an *Eye control* option. Here you can turn on eye control if you have compatible hardware, and you can choose which apps are allowed to use the eye tracker on your computer.

Using Voice Typing in Windows 11

If you have difficulty using a keyboard, or just cannot use a keyboard, you can dictate what you want Windows 11 and your apps to do and type using Voice typing. This doesn't need to be turned on in Settings and can be activated at any time by pressing the *Windows key + H* on your keyboard.

You will see a control bar appear at the bottom center of your screen in which you can click the *microphone* icon to start dictation, and the *settings* icon to turn on features such as auto-punctuation, see Figure 6-6.

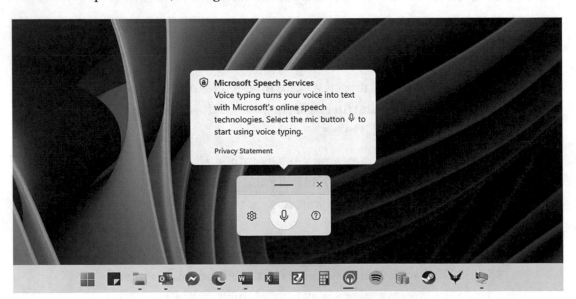

Figure 6-6. *You can dictate text and commands to Windows 11*

While dictation is useful for typing within apps, it's not usable for controlling windows itself. In the Accessibility settings under *Speech*, you will also find a *Voice access* control. You can activate this to allow you to control Windows by talking to your PC. Once activated, you will be shown a tutorial of how to use the feature, and it supports more than 80 spoken commands.

Make Windows 11 Easier to See

At the beginning of this chapter, I wrote about having to scale up the display on my laptop so that I can see anything. This is actually so commonly used that it's not part of the Accessibility settings at all, and your display might already be scaled without you even knowing it.

In Settings select *System* and then *Display*, and you will see a *Scale* option. This is a drop-down menu that will allow you to change the scale of text, icons, Start Menu, and Taskbar and buttons on your desktop from 100% (the full resolution of the monitor) all the way up to 250% or the maximum your screen size will support, see Figure 6-7.

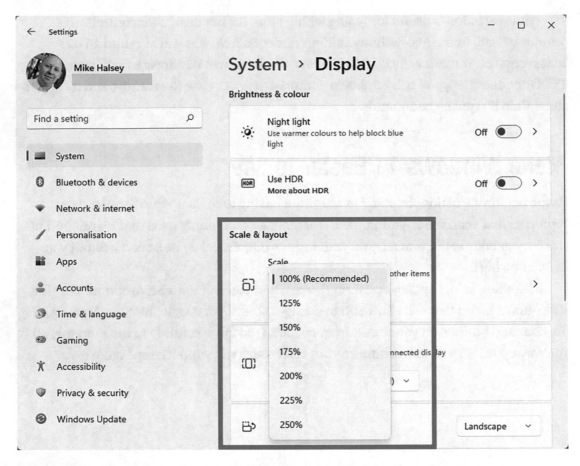

Figure 6-7. *You can scale your display from 100% right up to 250%*

Tip   If you want to make websites easier to see and use, you can click the *Zoom –* and + buttons in the drop-down menu in Edge, or press *Ctrl + Minus (-)* and *Ctrl + Plus (+)* to zoom into and out of web pages. This is remembered on a site by site basis and can be reset to normal by pressing *Ctrl + Zero (0)*.

Making Text Easier to Read

You might find though that all you need is to make text easier to read, I know I certainly do sometimes. In the Accessibility settings, click *Text size*, and you will find an easy-to-use slider control that will let you change the standard text size as it appears on the desktop and in your apps. You will see a preview of how text will appear above the slider to help you choose the correct setting.

Windows Narrator

If you have difficulty reading what is on your screen, or cannot read what's on the screen at all, you can activate the Narrator. Found in the Accessibility settings under *Narrator*, this will read everything on your screen in the active window and will also read things that you click on with your mouse. After you activate the Narrator, whatever it is that is being read on your screen is highlighted with a colored outline.

Microsoft Edge Browser Immersive Reader

If you find some web pages difficult to read, perhaps because there are too many distracting adverts, click the *Immersive Reader* button in the top right of the address bar. This will display the page as text and images only, with the adverts and other distractions filtered out. A new toolbar will appear at the top of the page that includes a *Read aloud* button you can click to have Windows 11 read the page contents to you.

Additionally, click the *Reading preferences* button on this toolbar, and you can activate *Line focus* mode. This will darken all of the pages except the current line (or three or five lines as you prefer) to help you concentrate on the content you are reading.

Tip   The Immersive Reader in Edge can also filter out the paywall functionality on some websites, allowing you to read the full content of their articles.

Changing Windows 11's Visual Effects

Things can go about pretty quickly on a PC desktop, from notifications that fly in and then fly back out again before you have a chance to read them to scrollbars that can be difficult to see, hard to grab, and annoying to use. In the Accessibility settings, click *Visual effects* and you can control all of this:

- **Always show scrollbars** makes the scrollbars in windows thicker and easier to see and grab and also displays them all of the time.

- **Transparency effects** turns the transparency in menus and windows on or off, which can make things easier to see on screen for some people.

- **Animation effects** is used to turn off animations such as opening, closing, and minimizing windows, and flyout notification popups, which some people can find distracting.

- **Dismiss notifications after** allows you to change how long notifications appear on your screen before they disappear. The default is 5 seconds, but you can increase this up to 15 or 30 seconds, or even 1 to 5 minutes.

The Windows Magnifier

The Magnifier in Windows has been around for many years now. It has been made largely redundant on the desktop, and text scaling options that have been introduced since, but is kept in Windows 11, both because some people find the text and desktop scaling options aren't enough for them and other people have grown accustomed to using it on their PCs, see Figure 6-8.

Figure 6-8. *The magnifier can make everything on your screen much larger*

Found in the Accessibility settings under *Magnifier*, it will display a control dock on your screen that allows you to set a zoom level, turn on narration, and select from three different magnifier types:

- **Docked** will display a permanently docked magnification panel at the top of your screen, leaving the rest of the screen at its normal resolution.

- **Full screen** zooms everything on the screen so the desktop appears to move around as you move your mouse cursor.

- **Lens** places a zoom lens underneath your mouse cursor which is like holding a magnifying glass over a newspaper as you read the text.

Windows 11 for Color-Blind People

If you are color-blind, you can sometimes find things on your screen difficult to see and read. In your daily life, you might have found placing a colored plastic sheet over text and images makes them easier to see, and Windows 11 includes a tool that simulates this.

Found in the Accessibility settings under *Color filters*, you can choose from *Red-green (green weak, deuteranopia)*, *Red-green (red weak, protanopia)*, *Blue-yellow (tritanopia)*, *Greyscale*, *Greyscale inverted*, and *Inverted* color filters, and everything you see on your screen will be tinted accordingly. At the top of the Color filters page is a live preview of colors and a picture so you can see what the effect of applying a filter will be.

Applying a High-Contrast Desktop Theme

In addition to the color filter and scaling options, you can also apply a high-contrast theme to everything on your desktop, which can make things easier to see for some people. In the Accessibility settings, click *Contrast themes* and you will see previews of four different theme types.

Below these is a drop-down menu where you can choose which one you want to use, *Aquatic*, *Desert*, *Dusk*, and *Night sky* (which rather makes them sound like scented candles; Ed), and then you click the *Apply* button to use the theme, see Figure 6-9.

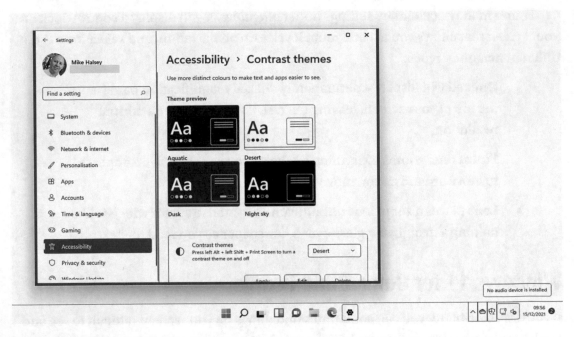

Figure 6-9. *You can apply high-contrast themes to your desktop*

These themes can also be personalized. Click the *Edit* button and you can change the different colors of items on your screen including text, links, and buttons.

Note   The visual accessibility features I am detailing in this chapter can be used together, so you can, for example, use a high-contrast theme and also use the color filter at the same time.

Make Windows 11 Easier to Hear

Sometimes you can miss important notifications or events on your PC because you can't hear them, or maybe can't enjoy music and video properly, because you have no or partial hearing in one ear. Windows 11 includes features that can be enormously helpful in this regard.

In the Accessibility settings, click *Audio* and all the options you need can be found in this one place. The first is that you can switch your sound in Windows 11 to *mono* audio. This might be useful if you have lost your hearing in one ear or have poor hearing in one ear and are watching video or listening to music.

Below this is an option to *Flash* [your] *screen during audio notifications*, see Figure 6-10.

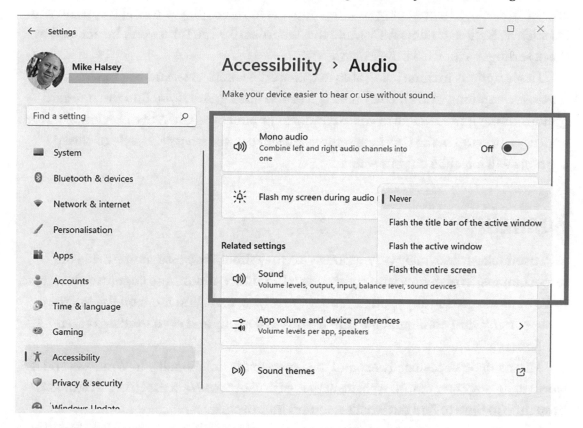

Figure 6-10. *You can make Windows 11 flash your screen during audio notifications*

These options can be useful for everybody from those with no or poor hearing to people that happen to work in a very noisy environment and/or might need to wear ear-defenders for their work, to people who have to work in a very quiet environment such as a library where people don't want to be disturbed by sounds from a PC. You can choose three different visual notification options:

- **Flash the title bar of the active window** which will flash the bar along the top of the window you are current using

- **Flash the active window** which will flash all four sides of the currently active window

- **Flash the entire screen** which will flash all your open windows and the desktop to alert you

Also available in the Accessibility settings is *Captions*. These options allow you to choose how closed-captioning subtitles appears in videos played through apps on your PC such as Netflix or Films & TV (note that websites like YouTube won't be affected by these settings as they have their own).

These options include being able to change the colors, size, and text font used for closed captions, and an *Edit* button gives you fine control if you find the standard options difficult to read due to color-blindness or poor eyesight. A live preview of a video appears at the top of the Captions settings, so you can see what each style of closed captions will look like on your screen.

Summary

Microsoft take accessibility very seriously, as they should because setting aside the important needs of people with special visual, auditory, motor, and cognitive challenges, none of us are getting any younger, and we're relying more and more on the Internet to shop, bank, and communicate with friends and family and even to access essential public services.

Microsoft do occasionally expand the accessibility functionality in Windows and it's worth checking their official website at `www.microsoft.com/Accessibility/windows` from time to time to find out what's new and improved.

Microsoft's main accessibility web page, `www.microsoft.com/accessibility`, also has links to how you can find and use accessibility features in the Microsoft 365 Office apps. You might also find their page on how they have made their Xbox games console accessible, useful as well. You can find this at `www.xbox.com/accessibility`.

In the next chapter, we will start to look at how you really get stuff done in Windows 11, and how you can use its productivity features to work more smartly and more effectively than you might realize.

CHAPTER 7

Being More Productive with Windows 11

We all like our smartphones, and many people enjoy using tablets such as the iPad, but when we look at the list of things we use these devices for, it's almost entirely based on the consumption of content rather than the creation of it. Reading web pages, shopping online, playing games, watching movies and TV shows, and using social media are all typical uses for such a device.

When we need to get things done however, we need a bigger and more flexible device. The reasons for this are simple, either we need a "proper" keyboard on which to type, we need more screen real-estate in which to be able to work, or we need something more powerful than a tablet to run the apps we need.

These things have always been the PC's greatest strengths. Modern tablets such as the iPad Pro are now able to replace our Windows laptops for getting some work done, but this is only because it has a laptop-sized screen, and when it's paired with a keyboard and a Bluetooth mouse. There is just no substitute for a full PC, and for any professional work, it's a desktop PC that will always win the day.

Fortunately, Windows 11 makes it really easy to be productive, with new features aimed to help you organize and manage your work and reduce the amount of stress and configuration that's required. In this chapter we'll look at all of these, and I'll show you how to become truly productive when using your Windows 11 PC.

Snap Layouts

Windows 7 introduced a feature called *Snap*, which meant that you could drag two of your on-screen windows to the far-left and the far-right sides of your screen, and they would snap there to both fill one half of the screen. Windows 10 expanded this to the four corners of the screen, but it was all far from ideal. It's still there if you want to use

© Mike Halsey 2022
M. Halsey, *Windows 11 Made Easy*, https://doi.org/10.1007/978-1-4842-8035-5_7

it should you want to, but rarely did the snap layouts it offered truly fit the window sizes you needed (though you could resize them in Windows 10), and it wasn't very discoverable.

Windows 11 has now introduced Snap Layouts, which fixed all of these problems. You will find it by hovering your mouse over the *Maximize* button in the top-right corner of any open window, see Figure 7-1.

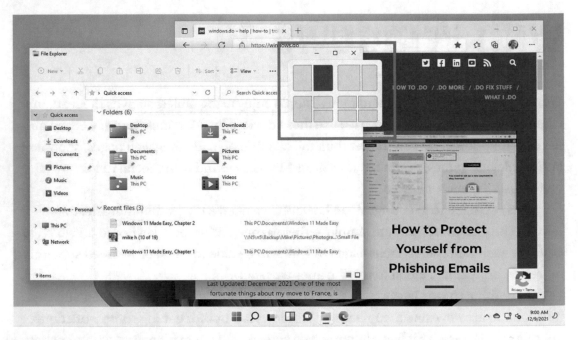

Figure 7-1. *Snap Layouts make it easy to arrange windows on your screen*

Doing this will display different layout options, and if you use a wider screen, more options will be available to you as Snap Layouts adapts to suit the screen size that you have.

Move your mouse over the layout designs to choose how you want that window to appear in your screen and click the appropriate box. The current window will then be snapped into that position and the remainder of the screen will highlight your other apps, so that you can choose which one or ones fill the remaining spaces, see Figure 7-2.

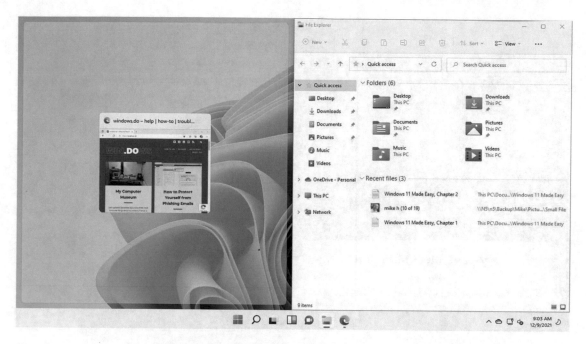

Figure 7-2. *Snap Layouts help you place your apps where you need them*

You can still resize your apps from there; moving your mouse cursor over the join between any apps will reveal a bar that you can drag to where you need it to be, allowing you to easily make apps large or smaller on the screen, see Figure 7-3.

Figure 7-3. *You can resize apps in Snap Layouts easily*

To remove an app from a Snap Layout, all you have to do is close it (when you're done with it obviously) or drag it out of position, at which point it will automatically return to the size and shape it was before you snapped it, so that you don't have to worry about making all your windows the size you want them to be again.

Tip   Windows 11 includes a feature I like to call "Boss Mode." If you move your mouse cursor to the very bottom-right corner of your desktop and click, all of the apps on your screen will be automatically minimized to the Taskbar. This can be very useful if you're doing something you perhaps shouldn't be (like playing Solitaire) when the boss walks past, though it is equally useful when shopping for a gift for someone who's in the house with you. If you click in the bottom-right corner of your screen again, all your windows will be restored to where they were before.

Using Multiple Desktops

Another feature that can be useful when the boss walks past is multiple desktops. This comes into its own when you want to separate different types of tasks, such a school or home working and gaming and browsing the Internet. To create a new desktop, click the *Task View* button on the Taskbar, which is the two overlapping squares to the right of the search icon.

This will display thumbnail images for all your running apps, but along the bottom of the screen will be representation of your current desktop, along with a *New Desktop* option to its right, see Figure 7-4.

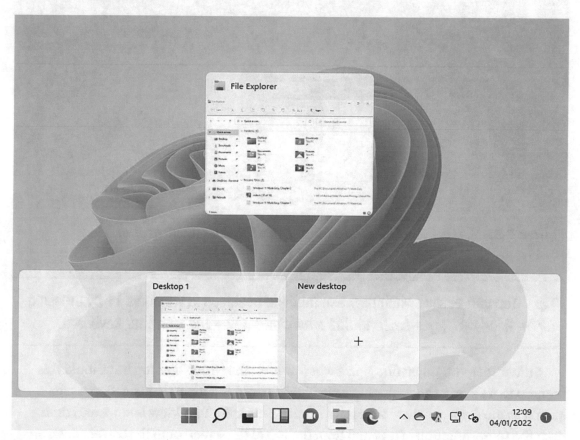

Figure 7-4. *You create new desktops by clicking the Task View button*

When you click to create a new desktop, this will be presented at the bottom of your screen next to the image of your fist desktop, and you can click between them to move from one desktop to another, see Figure 7-5.

Figure 7-5. *You access all your desktops from the Task View button*

Tip   You can easily switch between multiple desktops in Windows 11 by pressing *Ctrl + Windows key + Left* and *Ctrl + Windows key + Right* on your keyboard.

Sometimes you might find that a window is on the wrong desktop but should this happen there's no need to close it, switch desktops, and reopen it. Instead, you can switch to the desktop where the app is running, click the Task View button, and then drag the representation of that app from the top of the screen onto the correct desktop, see Figure 7-6.

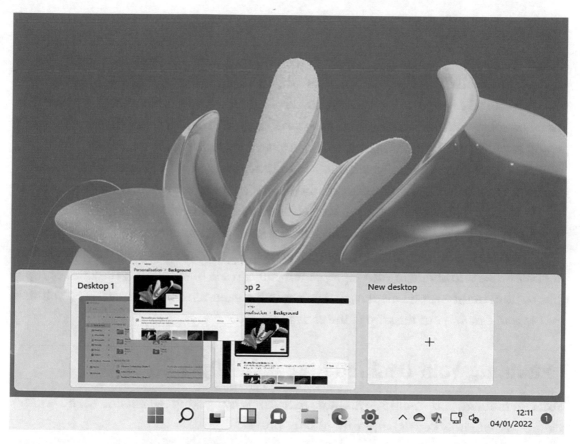

Figure 7-6. *You can drag and drop windows from one desktop to another*

You will have seen from the previous two images that each desktop can be customized with its own wallpaper. This can help you create environments that feel genuinely different from one another, to help you separate working from gaming.

Note   You can close a desktop in Task View by clicking the close icon in the top-right corner of its thumbnail display. Any apps open on that desktop will automatically be transferred to your main desktop.

Using Multiple Displays

One of the challenges of home working is the limited amount of screen real-estate you can get on a modern laptop. My own laptop has a 13-inch display, and if I needed to work on this all day every day, I would quickly find myself getting frustrated. This is why many people working from home on a laptop like to have a desk space they can use on which is a full-size PC monitor, and perhaps even a separate keyboard and mouse.

All of this allows you to stretch out, relax a little, and certainly avoid the bad posture problems that can come from being hunched over a laptop the whole time. Windows 11 handles multiple-monitor setups in very clever ways. When you plug in a second screen to your laptop (or desktop PC), you will first see your desktop copied on the new screen.

This is great for many people, though if your monitor is a slightly different resolution or screen size and shape to your laptop, then you can see black bars on the sides or top and bottom of the second display, which is wasting valuable desktop space. The solution to this is to *extend* your desktop to the second screen.

Extending Your Desktop Across Multiple Displays

You can manage your multiple monitors in Settings by clicking *System* and then *Display* where you will now see the multi-monitor controls.

Tip   You can get straight to the multi-monitor controls by right-clicking in a blank space on your desktop and selecting *Display settings* from the menu that appears.

Below and to the right of the representation of your monitors in Settings is a dropdown menu where you choose how your desktop is displayed across the multiple screens. Here you can choose to *extend* your desktop across the different displays, see Figure 7-7.

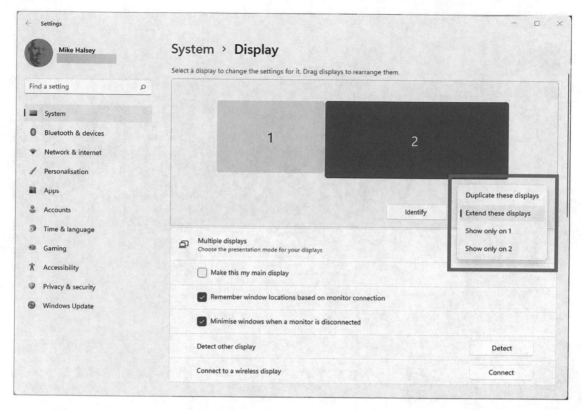

Figure 7-7. *You can extend your desktop across multiple monitors*

Below and to the right of the representation of your monitors in Settings is a dropdown menu where you choose how your desktop is displayed across the multiple screens.

Arranging Multiple Desktops on Your Monitors

You might find however that the representation of the displays in Settings doesn't match the physical layout of the monitors on your desk. This is easy to fix as these graphical representations of your monitors can be dragged around in the Settings panel and dropped where you need them to be.

To help you identify which monitor is which, there is an *identify* button below the representation of your monitors, see Figure 7-8. This will place a large number in the bottom-left corner of each display that will correspond to the number they are given in Settings. This can be especially helpful if you are using multiple monitors that are all the same size, shape, and resolution.

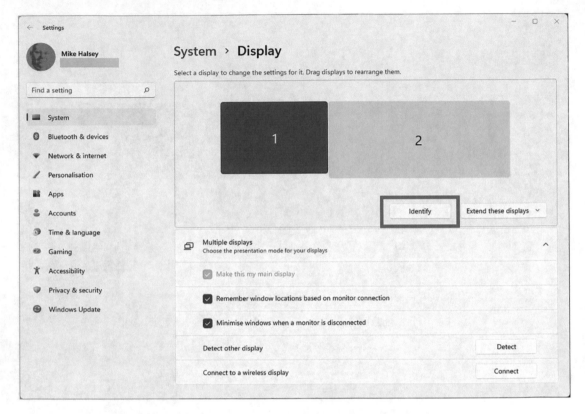

Figure 7-8. *Windows makes it each to identify each monitor*

You might find after doing this that monitor one is shown in Settings to be to the left of monitor two, when in fact the placement on your desk is different, perhaps with it being on the other side, or even above the other screen.

You can fix this easily by dragging the representations of your screens around in Settings until they are in the correct place. This means that when you extend your desktop, important things like the Taskbar and mouse cursor will always appear in the correct place.

Configuring Multiple-Monitor Settings

Below the representations of your monitors are three checkboxes, two of which provide some highly useful functionality. The first will let you click a monitor representation and select this as your *main display*. This means this will be the monitor on which your Start Menu will open.

Below this are two highly useful options. *Remember window locations based on monitor connection* and *Minimize windows when a monitor is disconnected*, see Figure 7-9.

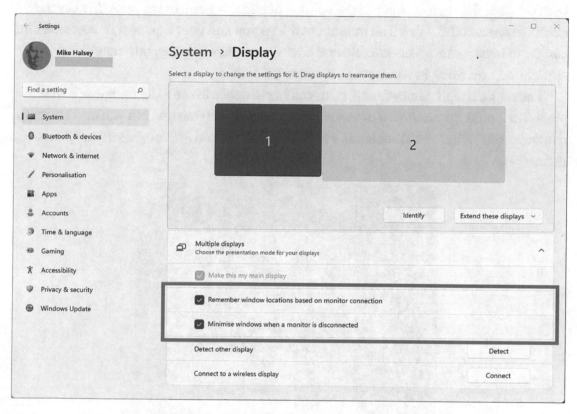

***Figure 7-9.** You can tell Windows to remember your window locations*

Let's deal with each one of these individually. One of the biggest problems in using a laptop with multiple monitors is rearranging all your apps after plugging the monitor into the PC. This setting, so long as you put your laptop to sleep instead or shutting it down, will remember where your apps were the last time you had that monitor connected, and if those apps are open on the PC, it will automatically place them back on the second screen where you had them before.

The second option help prevent a messy and cluttered desktop when you unplug the second screen by automatically minimizing any apps that were open on that screen. This can be very helpful as some apps might have had a window larger than would fit on your laptop's screen, and it also makes sure you don't suddenly find yourself with a laptop cluttered with open windows.

Saving the Planet by Printing to PDF

We all need to print a document from time to time, but there are problems associated with this, not the least of which is the volume of paper we use. In my book *The Green IT Guide (Apress, 2022)*, I detail all manner of things you and your business or organization can do to become more sustainable and environmentally friendly, but there's one straightforward thing in Windows 11 that can help.

Let's say a friend, family member, or colleague needs to see a document or a web page. You could print it for them so they can read it at their leisure, but you don't want to use the paper. Windows 11 includes a built-in printer called *Microsoft Print to PDF*, see Figure 7-10.

Figure 7-10. *Windows 11 lets you print documents as PDF files*

PDF (Portable Document Format) is a standard for electronic documents, and they can be read on every computing device, from smartphones and Google Chromebooks to PCs and Apple MacBooks.

Printing a document as a PDF saves the printed output as a file on your PC that you can then send to another person as an email attachment or via a messaging app.

Take Screenshots of Full Web Pages

On the subject of printing, sometimes you want to take an image of a web page, but the content you need to capture goes off the bottom of the visible page in your web browser. This can be frustrating, but Microsoft's Edge web browser has an in-built solution.

Open the options menu in Edge by clicking the three horizontal dots near the top-right corner of the browser window and select *Web capture*. You will see a dialog appear asking if you want to *Capture* [an] *area* or Capture *[the] full page*, see Figure 7-11.

Figure 7-11. You can screenshot whole web pages in Edge

If you chose the second option, the whole web page will be captured as an image, and you will see an option to *Save* the captured image, as well as add it to a Collection in Edge, something I detailed in Chapter 3, and to annotate the image by writing and drawing on it, see Figure 7-12.

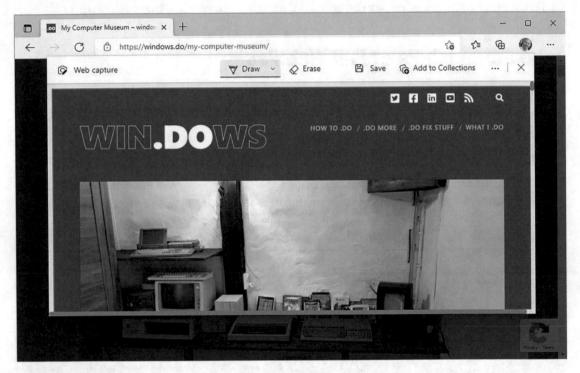

Figure 7-12. *You can save a whole web page as an image*

Using Pen and Ink with Windows 11

Annotating images brings me very neatly on the subject of using a pen with Windows, if your device supports pen usage, such as with the Microsoft Surface Pro devices. When you use a pen with Windows 11, you will see a pen tools icon appear in the system tray. Clicking this will display a pop-up menu with an app quick launcher, pre-populated with a few pen-friendly apps, see Figure 7-13.

Figure 7-13. *You can access the pen options from the System Tray*

If you click the *Settings* (cog or gear) icon in the pen options, you will see a menu appear in which you can *Edit* [the] *pen menu* or open the *Pen settings*. This first option will display a list of apps you can add to this pen quick launcher. You can click the *plus* (+) icon to their right to add them to the pen and ink quick launch menu, see Figure 7-14.

Figure 7-14. *You can choose more apps to use your pen with*

Alternatively, clicking *Pen settings* will open the full pen and ink settings for your PC, see Figure 7-15. Here you can control what any buttons on your pen do, and tell Windows if you are left- or right-handed, which is used to help configure palm rejection on your screen.

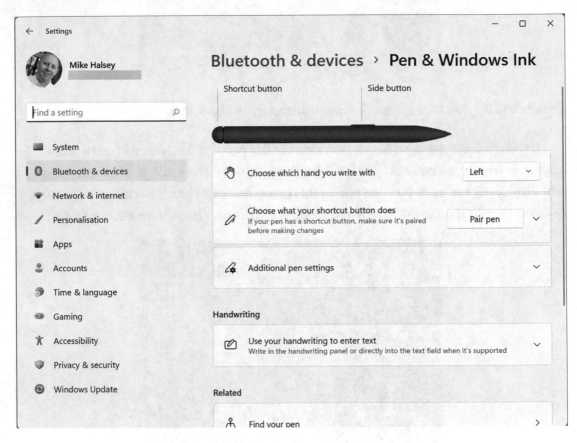

Figure 7-15. *Settings contains the main pen options*

Tip   Many apps support pen input, including Microsoft Office. It is well worth spending some time checking for pen support in your most used apps to see what additional functionality might be available to you.

There is also an *Additional pen settings* option which will open additional settings for pen use, see Figure 7-16. These settings may vary however depending on what pen you use and what its functionality is, so what you see might differ from what is shown here.

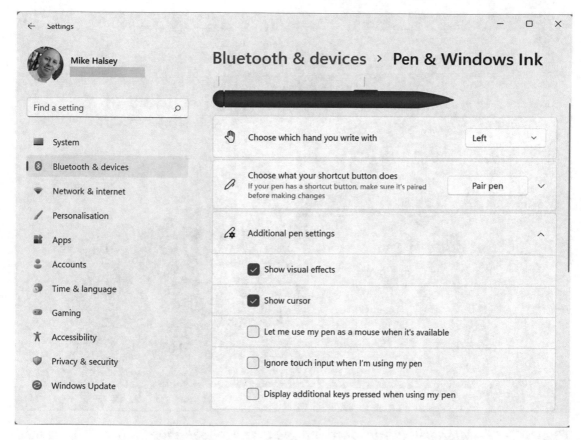

Figure 7-16. *The options you see may vary depending on what pen you use*

Microsoft Whiteboard

Not a part of all Windows 11 installations, though it will come with some pen-supporting PCs, Whiteboard is a fantastic app for collaboration and meetings and is available to download from the Microsoft Store.

Whiteboard is exactly what you might expect it to be, a digital, interactive whiteboard on which you can place text, images, and sticky notes (more on these shortly) and on which you can plan and demonstrate ideas collaboratively with other people in real time, all sharing the same whiteboard space, see Figure 7-17.

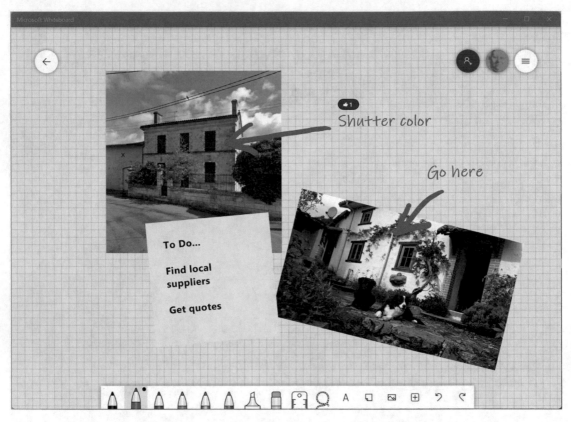

Figure 7-17. *Microsoft Whiteboard is a great app for collaboration*

As you might imagine, Whiteboard really comes into its own when used with a pen, and the canvas size is not limited by your screen, as you can drag it around to your heart's content.

I won't detail the functionality of Whiteboard too much because as I write this, Microsoft are in the process of overhauling it, so what you see will very likely look slightly different to what you see here, but the core functionality will remain the same.

Sticky Notes

I mentioned Sticky Notes a little while ago, and Windows 11 does come with a really useful Sticky Notes app that you can find by searching for it in the Start Menu. If you sign into Sticky Notes using a Microsoft Account or an Azure AD account from your organization, you can synchronize your sticky notes across PCs.

It does get better than this however as the Microsoft Office apps for Google's Android smartphone operating system, and for Apple's iOS on iPhones and iPads, also supports Sticky Notes, and you can synchronize your notes across all those devices too.

Sticky Notes are opened from the main Sticky Notes window, or from any note by clicking the *New Note* (+) button in the top-left corner. You can then type, write, and add images to your notes, see Figure 7-18.

Figure 7-18. *Sticky notes can be synced across PCs, tablets, and smartphones*

When you click on a Sticky Note, various options appear including being able to format text, or add images to the note, which appear across the bottom of the note, see Figure 7-19.

Figure 7-19. *You can add text or images to a Sticky Note*

If you click the three dots menu icon near the top left of the Sticky Note, you can change the color of the sticky note, delete that note, and also open the complete notes list, just in case you close it and can't find it again, see Figure 7-20.

Figure 7-20. *You can change the color of Sticky Notes*

Focus Assist

Despite all the tools and features in Windows 11 that can help you become more productive, there are still distractions in the world. That's why Windows 11 includes a feature called *Focus Assist*. This is easily activated from the Quick Settings menu on the Taskbar, see Figure 7-21.

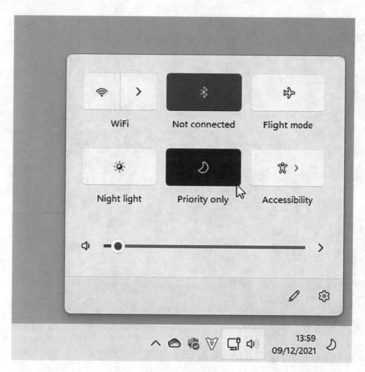

Figure 7-21. *Focus Assist is activated from the Quick Settings menu*

What Focus Assist does is to silence anything coming in that you might not want to be disturbed by, such as email and messaging notifications. If you open Settings and click *Focus Assist*, you can get finer control, such as being able to automatically activate the feature at certain times of the day, and on specific days of the week, see Figure 7-22.

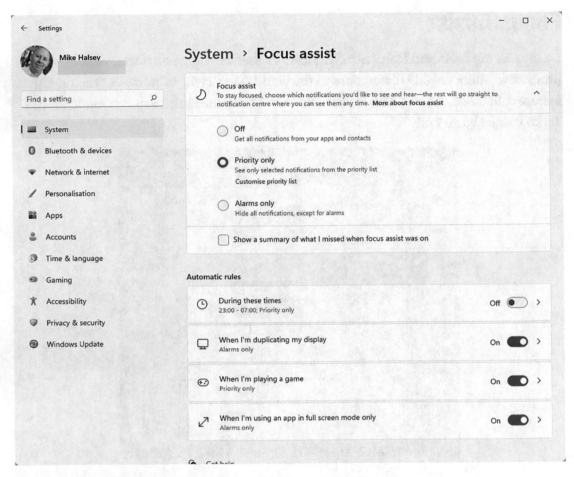

Figure 7-22. *You can configure Focus Assist in Settings*

There are also automatic rules you can deactivate if you wish, such as turning on Focus Assist if you are playing a game, or when using an app on your monitor full screen. This is a great way to keep your mind focused on the task at hand without distractions.

Summary

There are a lot of tools and functions built into Windows 11 that can help you to become more productive, and this is doubly important when you work from home and might also have distractions around you like children.

Work is very important though, and if you do work from home or use your PC for study, I will show you in the next chapter how to connect to your workplace or school and how you can get started using Microsoft Office.

CHAPTER 8

Getting Work Done

"The times, they are a-changin'" as Bob Dylan famously sang, and this would be true even if a certain global pandemic hadn't forced most people to work at home for more than a year. For some time now, there has been an appetite for people to want to work from home, or at least away from the workplace, wherever possible (I will put my hand up and admit I was always somebody who grabbed the opportunity to get out of the office for a day to relieve the monotony).

Perhaps fortuitously, advances in technology in the last few years have enabled working from home, sometimes called hybrid-working, in a way never considered possible before. Let me give you a few examples. Microsoft Teams, the company's online video meetings, messaging, and collaboration service launched in 2016. The Zoom video-conferencing app launched in 2012, and Microsoft's Azure, the company's business cloud-computing platform, launched in 2008.

Naturally, it took some time for these services to mature and reach a point where they were in common usage across businesses worldwide, and by the time 2019 came around, people in businesses and organizations were accustomed to using these services as part of their daily workflow.

Then we got the rollout of fiber broadband across countries, enabling households to often get faster Internet connections than their workplaces, and PCs were becoming faster and much more powerful, with Office 365 services even being accessible on iPads, Google Chromebooks, and Apple MacBook laptops.

Needless to say, by the time the global pandemic hit, the world was already well prepared to work from home. Had those problems hit us just a few years earlier, it would have been a struggle, and had the problems hit ten years earlier, then it would have been very difficult indeed.

© Mike Halsey 2022
M. Halsey, *Windows 11 Made Easy*, https://doi.org/10.1007/978-1-4842-8035-5_8

Connect to Your School or Workplace

Whether you're working from home for your job or your education, you can connect to your workplace with Windows 11 in the same way. Open *Settings* and navigate to *Accounts* and then *Email & accounts*. Here you will see a link called *Add a workplace or school account*. Clicking this will open a dialog in which you can add the email address or phone number associated with your own account with that organization, see Figure 8-1.

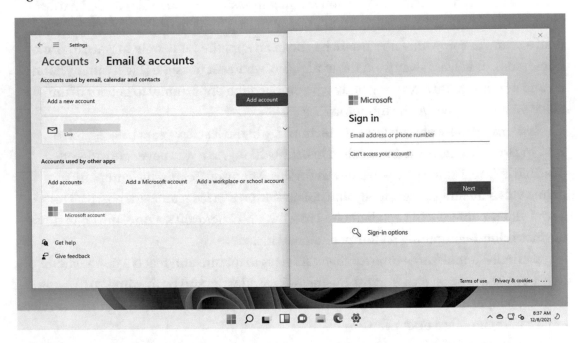

Figure 8-1. *You can sign into your school or workplace account in Settings*

Sometimes though you might not be sure what to type here, so you can search for your organization online instead; click the *Sign-in options* button at the bottom of the dialog window and you will see two more options: *Sign in with Windows Hello or a security key*, which you should use if your organization has provided you with an encrypted USB flash drive containing your sign-in credentials, and *Sign in to an organization*, where you can search for the organization "domain name," see Figure 8-2, which is another word to describe their business website address, such as **contoso.com**.

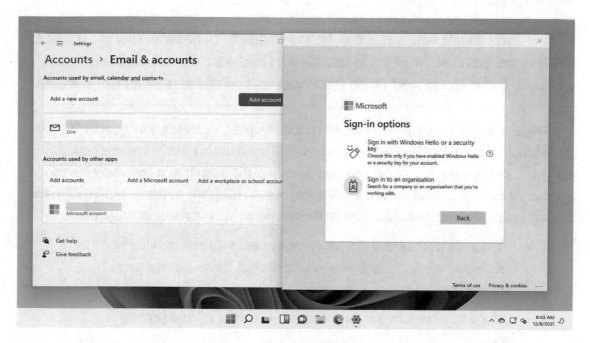

Figure 8-2. *You can search for your organization domain name to sign in*

How School and Workplace Sign-ins Affect Your PC

I want to put in a note here about how workplace and school sign-ins work on and affect your PC, as you might have been given a whole lot of rules you need to follow in order to get access.

Modern workplace sign-ins from your PC are designed to protect the organization's file shares, servers, and services from attack by malware, and from misuse by anyone who might have access to your PC and want to misbehave.

This means that you will very likely have to type your full password, which can often be long and complex, each time you sign into the organization's services. You could be prompted to set up Windows Hello on your PC. This is where you can sign in using facial recognition built into your webcam, or by a fingerprint reader in your laptop, though you will need compatible hardware for these to work. I will show you how to set up Windows Hello in Chapter 9.

> **Tip**   If you do not have a Windows Hello compatible device with your PC, the best way to get this functionality is to purchase a *Windows Hello compatible webcam*. You can find these at most online electronics and computer retailers and in stores.

Depending on how your organization has set up their access security, your PC will need to conform to certain standards which will most likely be activated automatically for you if they are not currently configured on your PC. You should not worry about your organization having some control over your PC however, as the things listed in the following are recommendations I make for you personally in this book regardless:

- Windows Update must be set to receive security and stability updates as they are distributed by Microsoft, though Feature packs may be deferred.

- Anti-Malware software must be present on the PC and kept up to date.

If your PC doesn't conform to these two rules, you may be denied access to your organization's servers until it is, but as I say, these can be configured for you automatically by the system, and they're both a good thing anyway.

One last thing to note is that your organization retains control over any files and documents that reside on your PC, but that belong to their organization. This means that even after you leave the company they can, through Windows internal systems, remotely wipe those files, documents, and online access accounts from your computer. They cannot however **ever** see or touch anything else.

> **Note**   If your organization uses Google Workspace, you may be required to download and install the Google Chrome web browser and sign into your organization's services through that instead of Settings. If you are unsure, ask your line manager or IT Helpdesk.

Setting Up Online Document Access

OneDrive is Microsoft's cloud file backup and sync service, and in Windows 11, you can have a personal account and a work account set up at the same time. This is easy to set up too, and I detailed how you can do this in Chapter 5.

If your organization uses Google's Workspace service, and you need to set up sync with Google Drive, you can download and install the file and document sync app from `www.google.com/drive/download`.

Setting Up Microsoft Teams

If your organization uses Microsoft Teams, you will find this app preinstalled in Windows 11. This is perhaps subject to change in the future should a third-party company such as Google, Slack, or Zoom complain to a regulatory body such as the European Union about this bundling, Microsoft could be forced to remove it later, but we'll see, for now it's still there.

Teams is pinned to the Start Menu when you first install Windows 11, making it very easy to find, and when you first click its icon, you will be invited to sign into the Microsoft Account you use with Windows 11, see Figure 8-3.

Figure 8-3. *Microsoft Teams is preinstalled in Windows 11*

Note   I would like to drop in a note about using Teams with your personal Microsoft Account. This can be very useful if you have family or friends you want to chat to, or share documents with in a safe and secure way. It's common for people to use Facebook Messenger or WhatsApp for such a task, but both these companies are owned by Meta (formerly Facebook) and that company, let's face it, doesn't have the greatest track-record on privacy as they sell advertising. Teams therefore can be a great alternative for private conversations, and it works with a Microsoft Family account if you have one.

You can sign into Teams using your organization's account by clicking the *Use another account* link at the bottom of the sign-in window. This will display a new dialog in which you can click *Use another account* (again) to sign into your work account if it is not already associated with your PC, see Figure 8-4. If you then need the full Teams app, a link at the bottom of the window will take you to it in the Microsoft Store so that you can download and install it.

Figure 8-4. *You can sign into a workplace Teams account*

Setting Up Microsoft Office

Microsoft's Office suite of apps is likely something you are already familiar with, with Word, Excel, PowerPoint, Outlook, and Access being a staple of home and workplace documents since they were first introduced in 1995. Microsoft Office isn't installed by default in Windows 11, though some PC manufacturers might preinstall it for you. If Word, Excel, and Outlook aren't installed and in the Start Menu on your PC, you will have an app called *Office*, see Figure 8-5. You will find it pinned to the Start Menu.

Figure 8-5. *Microsoft Office is preinstalled in Windows 11*

Opening the *Office* app will show you automatically signed into your personal Microsoft Account if that's what you have used to sign into Windows 11, and you will see a list of your recently accessed documents, with quick links on the left to cut-down versions of Word, Excel, and PowerPoint, which run in the Office app window, see Figure 8-6.

Figure 8-6. *You can install full Microsoft Office through the Office app*

Near the top-right corner of the Office app window is a link to *Install Office,* and you can click this to sign into your Microsoft 365 or workplace Azure AD account online and download the full Office suite of apps to install.

Managing Accounts in Microsoft Office

In the very top-right corner of the Office app window is your avatar, and clicking this will display options to sign into Office with a different account, see Figure 8-7. Clicking *Switch account* will display a dialog where you can choose a different Microsoft Account to sign into or choose a *Workplace or school account* instead.

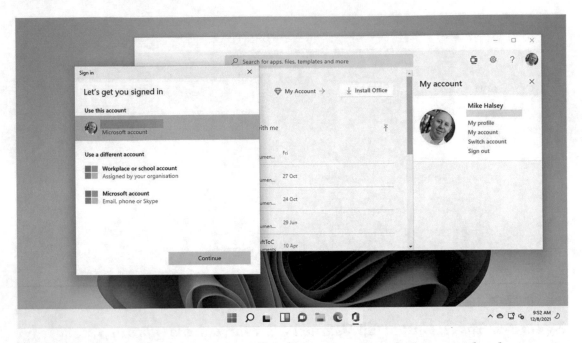

Figure 8-7. *You can sign into the Office App using a workplace or school account*

When you have the full suite of Microsoft Office apps installed on your PC, you can open one and sign in. When you have signed into one of the Office apps, you will be automatically signed into all the others. At the top center of each of the Office apps, in Figure 8-8, you can see am I using Excel, you will see your name and avatar. Clicking this will allow you to sign into an account, or switch between home and workplace accounts.

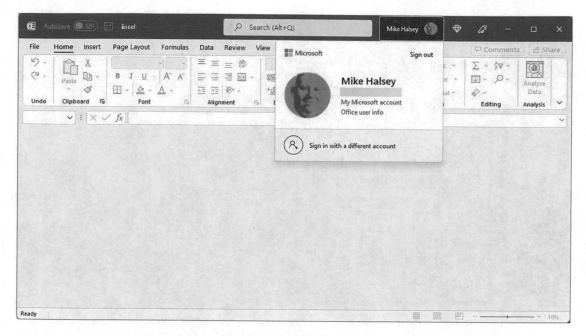

Figure 8-8. *You can sign into and switch between accounts in all Office apps*

When you are using Word, Excel, PowerPoint, Outlook, and the other Office apps, clicking the *File* menu will display options for creating and opening documents, and for managing your account. Click *Account* in the bottom-left corner of the window and you will see options to switch to a different Microsoft or workplace account, if you need to, and to connect additional service to Office such as OneDrive for Business, or Google Drive, see Figure 8-9.

Figure 8-9. *You can connect services including OneDrive for Business to Office*

Tip   You can personalize the look and feel of Microsoft Office to make it more pleasant for you to work with. You do this from the *File* menu and then clicking *Account*. Here you will see options to change the *Office Background* and the *Office Theme*, as seen in Figure 8-9.

Summary

Windows 11 makes it very easy for you to get connected to your school or workplace, and very easy to manage and switch between work and personal accounts in Microsoft Office, along with giving your organization the peace of mind that you're doing so safely and securely.

This brings us neatly onto the subject we'll look at in the next chapter, where we'll look in depth at how you can manage and secure your privacy and security on your Windows 11 PCs.

CHAPTER 9

Managing Your Privacy and Security

In Chapter 3, I showed you how to get online with Windows 11, and I also showed you some of the things you can do with Microsoft's Edge web browser to stay safe whatever you're doing on the Internet. It's true that when we shop, bank, or share files and documents, there are always criminals that want in; they want to steal your credit card and banking information, your usernames and passwords, and to infect your files and documents with malware and even ransomware.

These aren't a problem though, as in this chapter, I'll teach you everything you need to do to set up your PCs in a worry-free way. There are other problems though that are really only starting to come to the public's attention. This is advertising and other companies that track us, compile detailed information about us, and use that information to sell it to advertisers, so we will part with our hard-earned cash to pay for products we probably don't need, and likely otherwise wouldn't purchase.

Fortunately, Windows 11 also includes features to help stop these trackers, and we'll also look at how to do that in this chapter.

Creating Secure Passwords

Let's start with protecting your PC or laptop from physical theft. The Federal Bureau of Investigation (FBI) estimates that some two million laptops are stolen in the United States every year and that 10% of laptops will be stolen in their first year of ownership, with only 3% of those being recovered.

Of the laptops and desktop PCs stolen, how many are using a password to sign in? One of the benefits of modern Windows is the convenience with being able to set a pin code to sign into your Microsoft Account. The problem comes when the total number of possible combinations for a pin are potentially less than 10,000 as we've all become

© Mike Halsey 2022
M. Halsey, *Windows 11 Made Easy*, https://doi.org/10.1007/978-1-4842-8035-5_9

used to using just four digits with our bank cards. When you compare this to the billions of combinations that come with setting a strong password, which Microsoft and other companies will at the very least strongly encourage when you create a new account or change your password, it's clear to see the chances of breaking into a user account on a PC with a pin isn't overly difficult.

Once a criminal has access to a PC, they will also have access to your email, social media account(s), and any stored usernames and passwords for websites, banking, and more.

This is *not*, I must stress, a reason to never store usernames and password on a PC. If you don't store usernames and passwords, the odds are highly likely those usernames and passwords will be fairly simple, easily guessable, and very short and insecure.

The idea then is to use a combination of factors to keep yourself and your data secure. The first of these is to create a strong password in the first instance, and you can check how secure your current password(s) is/are at `www.security.org/how-secure-is-my-password`.

The most insecure passwords in use today are also the most easily guessable because they're also the most commonly used passwords. These are always the ones criminals will try first. Is one or more of your passwords in this list?

- 123456
- 123456789
- 12345
- qwerty
- password
- qwerty123
- 000000
- 1q2w3e
- password1

There are also other commonly used passwords such as *monkey, iloveyou, letmein,* and *trustno1*. If you recognize any of these passwords, or even use them yourself, you should change them straightaway.

How Do You Choose a Strong, Easy to Remember Password?

Let's start by what you should definitely not use in your password or your username:

- Your date of birth, or part of it

- The name of a family member or child

- The name of a pet

- Your own name

- Easily guessable information such as where you work

- Personal information such as where you were born or your maiden (unmarried) surname

The best passwords are made from phrases and sentences, such as a quote from your favorite book or TV show. These passwords are secure because they are long. I want to use one as an example; we'll see how we can make it more secure.

Let's start with the phrase "space the final frontier" from Star Trek. First, we remove the spaces but leave in capital letters.

- SpaceTheFinalFrontier

  Next, we will replace some letters with numbers, but just the ones that are easy to identify and remember, so swapping an F for the number 5, and an i for the number 1.

- SpaceThe51nal5ront1er

  Lastly, we'll replace more letters with symbols, but again only ones that can be easily remembered, so we'll replace the letter o with open and close brackets () and the letter a with the pound (hash) symbol.

- Sp#ceThe51n#l5r()nt1er

  The second password is significantly more secure than the first while being easy to remember as you're only using two numbers, 1 and 5, instead of letters. The last password, again using only two symbols, appears almost completely random.

Using a Password Manager

Windows 11's Edge browser and all other web browsers including Google Chrome include a password manager. These include functionality including remembering your passwords for you, autofilling online forms with your passwords, generating strong passwords for you, and alerting you when your passwords have been found out in the wild.

You can get additional functionality through from a dedicated password manager, and I personally use LastPass (`www.lastpass.com`), though many others are available. These password managers aren't usually free to use, but they do offer enhanced functionality.

One of perhaps the greatest benefits to using a password manager is being able to share your usernames and passwords with friends and family. This can be useful if, to give one example, you are temporarily incapacitated through illness or injury but need to access to online accounts to transfer money, pay bills, or purchase items and food for your family.

Using Two-Factor Authentication

Most online and web services these days offer two-factor authentication (TFA), sometimes called multifactor authentication, as a means of further security of your account. These are, slowly but surely, getting more clever and useful. The most basic TFA services require a cellphone they will send a code to over SMS. This is perhaps the least useful as, I don't know about you, but I don't like being tied to my smartphone any more so it is frequently in a drawer, or even in the wrong building when a code comes through.

Others will allow the sending of the code to your email address. I personally find this very useful purely because it offers me a way to receive the security code when my smartphone isn't to hand.

The best TFA solutions will use an authenticator app, such as the Microsoft Authenticator app, which you can find in the Google Play and Apple iOS stores. These can be set up for your online accounts and will either generate a short code you type into a website to confirm it's you, or will pop up an alert that you can simply tap to approve.

These TFA apps are doubly secure because they work with the biometric security available on modern smartphones, where you use your face or fingerprint to sign in. If you have not set biometrics on your smartphone, I highly recommend it as even the most fastidious person can lose their phone, and these biometric systems are commonly built into the power button on the device anyway.

Setting Up Windows Hello

Windows Hello is supported on many laptops and can be relatively easily be added to desktop PCs. It requires either a compatible webcam (which you can purchase from online or retail stores for desktop PCs) or a fingerprint reader.

You can find Windows Hello in Settings, under *Accounts* and then *Sign-in options*. If you have any Windows Hello compatible devices in your PC, you will see the biometric options showing as available, see Figure 9-1.

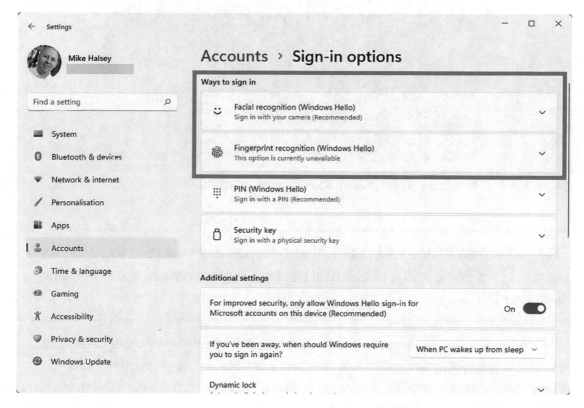

Figure 9-1. You can set up Windows Hello in Settings

When you set up Windows Hello, you will be asked to place one or more fingers on the PC's fingerprint reader, if you are using one, or to look into your biometric camera, see Figure 9-2.

Figure 9-2. *Windows Hello is easy to set up on your PC*

Tip   If you use a fingerprint reader, always register more than one finger or thumb as a cut on a finger with a plaster on it can be enough to prevent you from signing into your PC.

Windows Hello has also started being used on PCs by third-party companies and services to help you quickly sign into their services with your fingerprint or facial recognition, which is another reason to set it up if your PC supports it, as this means you often won't need an authenticator app.

Setting Up Find My Device

Earlier in this chapter, I talked about how many laptops are stolen every year and how few of them are ever recovered. Windows 11 includes a useful feature called "Find my device" which you can activate to help you track down your laptop if you are ever unfortunate enough to lose it. You can set this feature up in Settings by navigating to *Privacy & security* and then *Find my device*, see Figure 9-3.

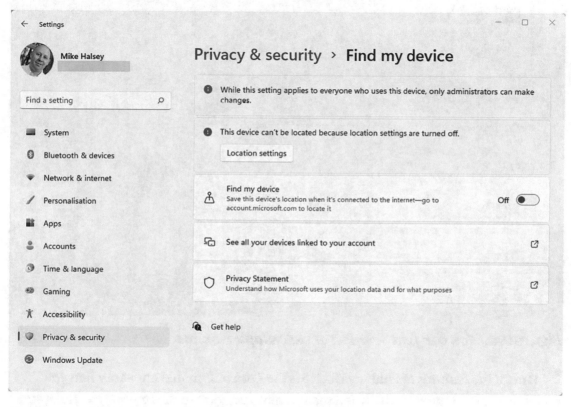

Figure 9-3. *You can set up Find my Device in Settings*

Should you lose your laptop, or have it stolen, you can go to any web browser and sign into your Microsoft Account, going to `https://account.microsoft.com/devices/ find-my-device` where a list of your PCs on which the feature is enabled will be displayed, see Figure 9-4.

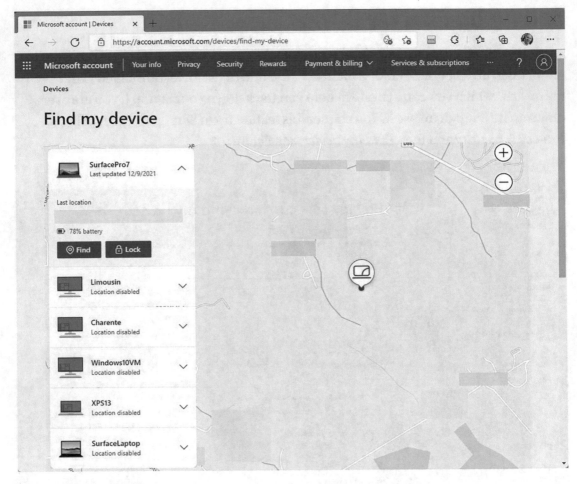

Figure 9-4. *You can find your lost or stolen laptop online*

One of the features of Find my Device is the *Lock* button that appears when you search for it. Clicking this will, when that PC next connects to the Internet, secure it so that nobody can access your account on the device.

The Windows Security Center

One of the problems with using computing devices of any kind is the threat of malware attacking and affecting the PC. Windows 11 comes with inbuilt protection that will effectively guard against threats. You can access it in one of three different ways.

Open Settings and navigate to *Privacy & security*, click *Windows Security*, see Figure 9-5, and then click the *Open Windows Security* button.

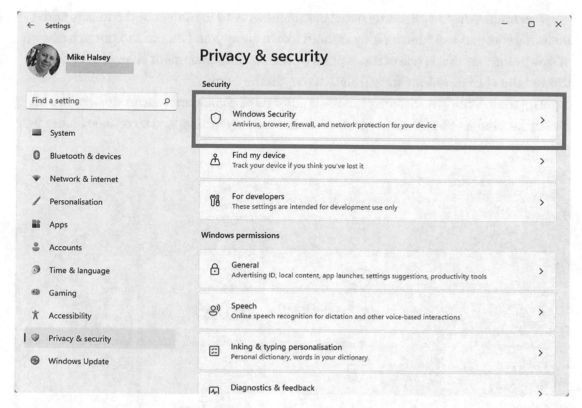

Figure 9-5. *You can open Windows Security from Settings*

The second way is to search in the Start Menu *all apps* list or to type a search in the Start Menu for **windows security** which will display it, so you can click it to open the panel.

The last way, and perhaps the easiest and most convenient, is to click the blue shield icon that sits in the Taskbar System Tray, see Figure 9-6. It may be hidden but click the small up (^) arrow to reveal any hidden icons.

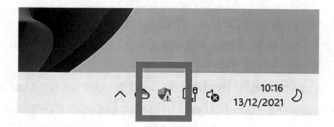

Figure 9-6. *You can open Windows Security from its System Tray icon*

The main Windows Security panel is straightforward to understand and use, and it includes some useful functionality I would like to show you. I do want to put in a caveat at this point that this is one of those parts of Windows 11 that might change over time, though the core functionality will always remain the same.

The main Windows Security interface consists of eight icons (currently) that are all clearly labeled as *Virus & threat protection*, *Account protection*, and so on, see Figure 9-7.

Figure 9-7. *Windows Security is straightforward to understand*

Virus and Threat Protection

If you want to perform a scan for malware, this is where you can do it, and you will see a button labeled *Quick Scan* as well as a *Scan options* link. There are two extremely useful features here that I want to highlight.

The first of these can be found by clicking *Scan options* and it is called *Microsoft Defender Offline scan*, see Figure 9-8. If you ever suspect your computer has been infected with malware, this is the tool to use. Malware likes to embed itself in the Windows startup files, so that when you start your computer from it being switched off, the malware starts immediately too.

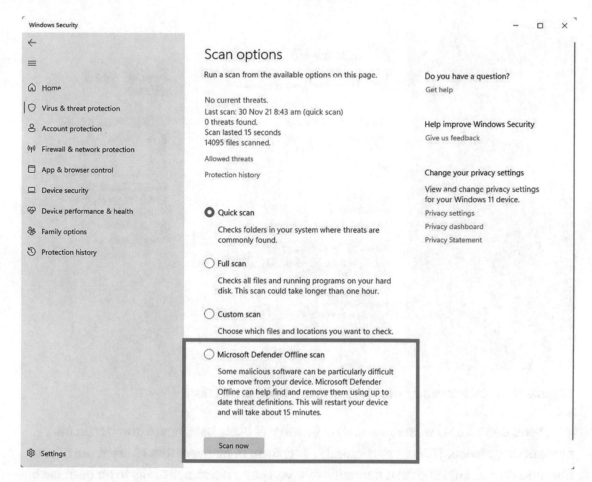

Figure 9-8. *Windows 11 can restart and perform an "offline" scan*

They do this because it commonly allows them to bypass the security and anti-malware systems in the operating system itself. When you perform a scan using Microsoft Defender Offline, your PC will restart, and the scan will take place without Windows (and the malware) being loaded.

The second feature I want to highlight is in the main *Virus & threat protection* panel. Scroll to the bottom of the page and you will see *Ransomware protection*. Click the *Manage ransomware protection* link to configure this option, see Figure 9-9.

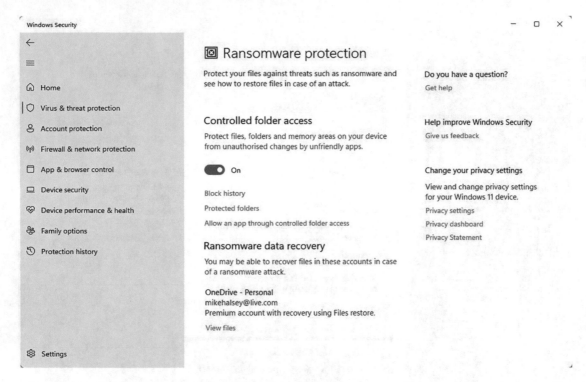

Figure 9-9. *Windows 11 includes ransomware protection*

If you don't know what ransomware is, you will likely have heard about it on the news once or twice. This is a particularly nasty form of malware that encrypts all of your files and documents and then demands that you pay a ransom, usually in an untraceable currency such as Bitcoin, to unlock the files.

Even if you do pay the ransom, which can be a considerable sum of money, there's no guarantee your files will be unlocked, and every chance the program the criminals give you to unlock the files will also contain its own malware payload.

This is where Windows 11's ransomware protection feature, called *Controlled folder access*, comes in useful. This feature monitors all of your user folders, and any additional folders and disks that you specify are to be protected (click the *Protected folders* link to add more), and if any software that's not been preinstalled or installed by yourself tries to change, delete, or encrypt any files, it stops that from happening.

There is a caveat with this I need to highlight. If you use your Windows 11 for routine tasks such as you just use a web browser, or Microsoft Office, then you should never notice it's even activated. If, however, you use any third-party software, you might on occasion get a false positive with Windows 11 blocking file and folder access for an installed app that actually needs it.

Should this happen, then you'll be immediately informed by a pop-up alert on your desktop, and it's easily fixed. In Windows Security, in the main *Virus & threat protection panel*, click the *Protection history* link. This will display a list of threats and false positives that have been found, and they're listed by date and time, so you'll easily be able to see which one is the most recent.

Click the event and you will see details about it including the *Affected items* which will tell you the name of the app that was blocked, see Figure 9-10.

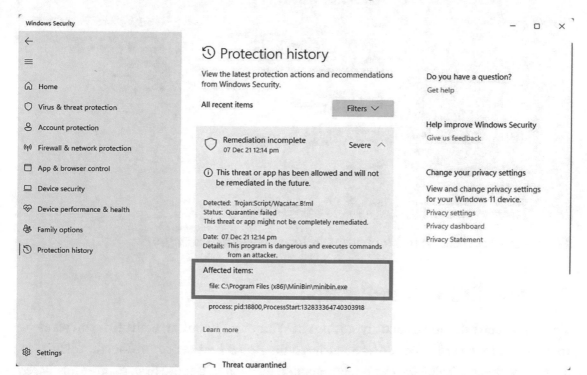

Figure 9-10. *You can fix false-positive app blocks*

You will also have an option to *Allow* that app, so the problem doesn't recur. Alternatively, on the *Ransomware protection* page, click the *Allow an app through controlled folder access* link, and you will see an *Add an allowed app* button. Click this and you will have two further options including being able to select an app on your PC, but to also select a *Recently blocked app*, see Figure 9-11.

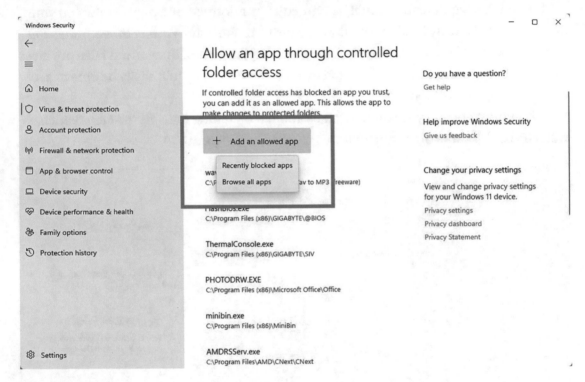

Figure 9-11. *You can unblock apps in Ransomware protection*

App and Browser Protection

There are also additional security settings in Windows 11 you can activate if you want to. Some of these are in Windows Security in the *App & browser control* section. The second of these, *Exploit protection*, is activated by default, but the first, *Reputation-based protection*, is something you can activate yourself, see Figure 9-12.

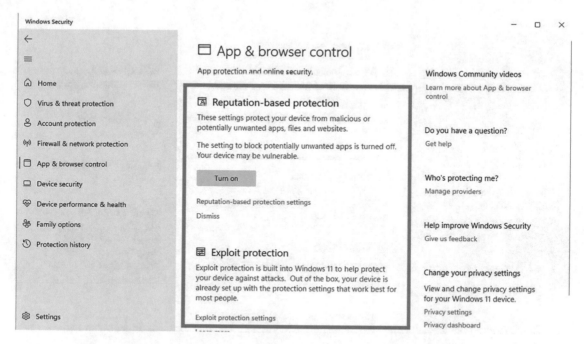

Figure 9-12.   You can activate reputation-based malware protection

This feature is disabled because it can, like the ransomware protection, interfere with a few apps you might want to use, but if you use mainly mainstream apps such as a web browser, Microsoft Office, and other well-known software such as Adobe Creative Cloud, then you will find the feature will give you added protection from malware while also staying out of your way.

Core Isolation

The last security feature I want to highlight is called *Core Isolation*, and it is also found in Windows Security, see Figure 9-13. This is again disabled by default as it can interfere with some apps, but if you turn it on and later find an app is misbehaving or not working, you can always turn it off again the same way. Core Isolation can prevent malware from placing itself into vulnerable areas of the PC's memory, which can bypass some security features.

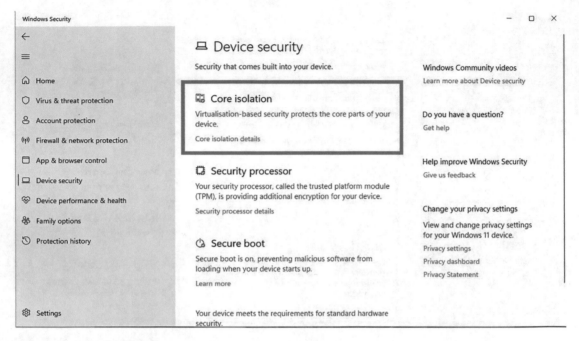

Figure 9-13. *Core isolation can stop malware infecting your PC*

Managing Your Privacy in Windows 11

Windows Settings also include a full set of privacy features that, as well as meaning your PC only sends the data to Microsoft that you approve of, can also prevent third-party apps from accessing your data, and even hardware such as your camera and microphone. These can be found under *Privacy & security* in the *Windows Permissions* section, see Figure 9-14.

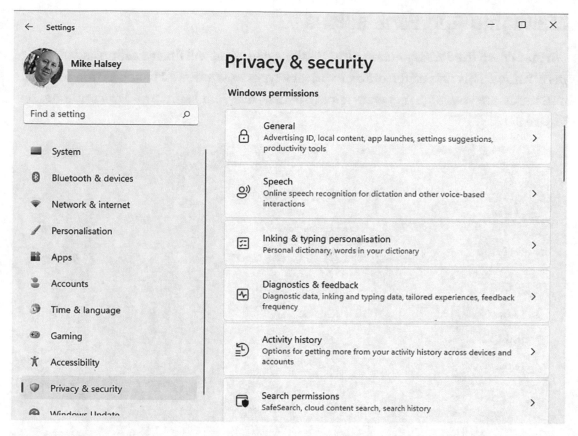

Figure 9-14. *You can set privacy permissions in Windows 11 Settings*

One of the things people can be concerned about is what data their PC sends to Microsoft (and equally what data their smartphone sends to Google or Apple). This is easy to control in Windows 11. In *Privacy & security,* click *Diagnostics & feedback,* and you will see an option to uncheck *Send optional diagnostic data.*

Note   It's worth discussing what data your PC sends to Microsoft and why as you can't opt out of some of it at all. This *required* data contains information of your hardware, installed software, and Windows installation that Windows Update must have in order to provide you with the best, and with appropriate security and stability updates, and hardware drivers. The *optional diagnostic data* is **anonymous** information about how you use your PC, and this is used by Microsoft to further refine the overall Windows 11 experience.

Managing App Permissions

Further down the *Privacy and security* Settings page, you will find a section called *App permissions*. This lists all the different privacy types in Windows 11 such as notifications, and hardware you might not want apps to access, like your camera and microphone, see Figure 9-15.

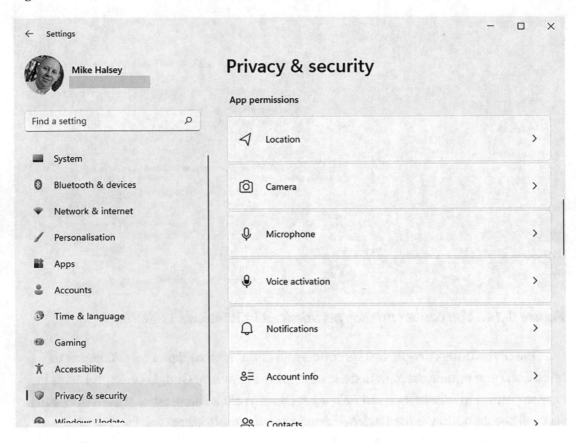

Figure 9-15. *You can control privacy for hardware in your PC*

Clicking any of these categories will display further privacy controls for that device or Windows feature, see Figure 9-16. It will also list all the installed apps that have permission to use that device or feature. You can click the switches to turn access for any app on or off and even disable that device entirely on your PC should you wish.

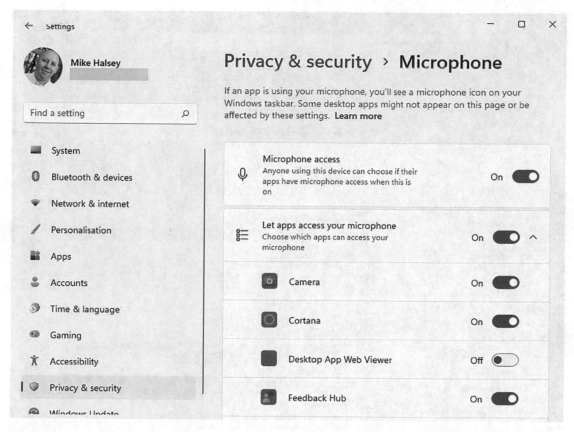

Figure 9-16. *You can disable permissions for any app in the Privacy settings*

Managing Privacy in Microsoft Edge

In Chapter 3, I showed you features in Microsoft's Edge web browser that you can use to manage and control your privacy online, but there's more control you still have and more you can do to improve your privacy online. Open Edge's Settings page by clicking the three horizontal dots near the top-right corner of the browser window and navigate to *Cookies and site permissions*.

This page falls in several categories, see Figure 9-17. At the top of the page is a *Manage and delete cookies and site data* option. If you have your privacy set to Strict as I detailed in Chapter 3, you should already have tracking and advertising cookies blocked in your browser. What remains are usually cookies that store your login and preference data for websites.

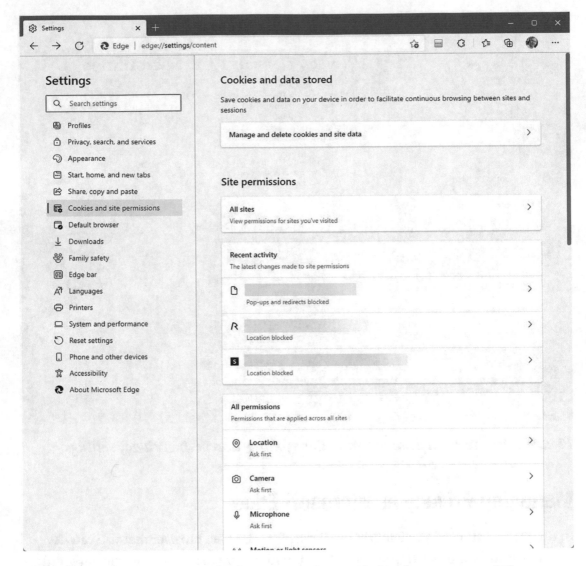

Figure 9-17. *You can control what permissions websites have on your PC*

In the *Site permissions* section, you will find specific permissions that have been granted to websites, such as accessing your location, see Figure 9-18. For some websites, this is actually necessary, such as an online meeting website like Skype or Zoom having access to your camera and microphone, but for others, you might want to remove access, which is often where a website wants to know your location.

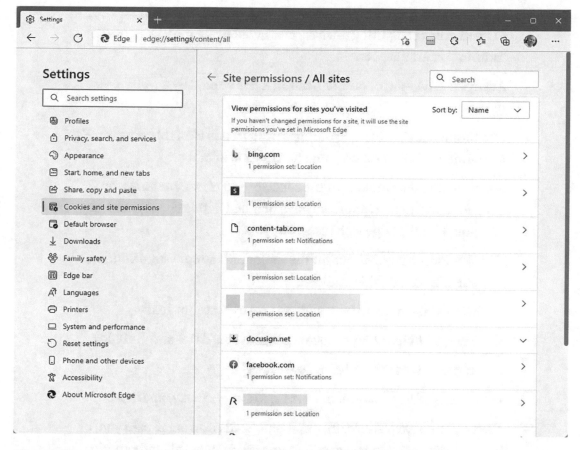

Figure 9-18. *You can remove website permissions in Edge*

At the bottom of the *Cookies and site permissions* settings in Edge are the same type of hardware and windows feature permissions that I detailed in Windows Settings, such as notifications and microphone. You can remove permission for individual websites or block all websites from getting access through a simple click of a switch.

Top Tips for Security and Staying Safe

So, what are my absolute top tips for staying safe online, and for keeping your privacy? These are all fairly simple and straightforward things to do, and I would recommend each and every one of them to be used by everybody.

- Create strong passwords for websites and web services and for your PC and other computing devices, and avoid using the username "admin" on any devices.

- Always use two-factor authentication if it is offered by a web service or device.

- Use biometric sign-in (face or fingerprint) if it is available on your PC, as Windows Hello, and on your smartphone or tablet.

- Spend a little time looking at the security and privacy settings for your PC and installed apps as I have detailed in this chapter and in Chapter 3 for the Edge web browser.

- Check your privacy settings for the major operating system vendors you use. You can do this online at

  - Microsoft - `https://account.microsoft.com/privacy`

  - Google - `https://myaccount.google.com/data-and-privacy`

  - Apple - `https://appleid.apple.com`

  - Amazon Alexa - `www.amazon.com/alexa-privacy/apd/home`

- Never give out your usernames and passwords if an email asks you, or if you receive a text message or a phone call asking you for them. No reputable website, online service or shopping website, and no bank or financial institution will *EVER* ask you to disclose this information.

- Never give out personal information that can be used to help criminals get access to your accounts; this includes your date of birth, maiden (unmarried) name, the names of your parents or children, place of birth, or name of your spouse or partner.

- Avoid answering seemingly innocent posts on social media that really exist to harvest your data, such as "What was the name of your first pet" or "What was the name of your first school." These are the answers to common security questions.

- Always keep a full backup copy of your files and documents, and an online service such as Microsoft OneDrive is perfectly acceptable for this.

Summary

It's only in recent years that people have really become aware of the privacy implications of using computers, smartphones, and the Internet. Some companies including Google and Facebook have been heavily criticized for the way their users have become a way to fund their lucrative advertising businesses, with the personal and activity data of each person having a tangible monetary value.

Fortunately, it's straightforward to control your privacy online, and also to keep your PC safe and secure from malware. The last thing you want to have to do is worry about everything you do, download, and click.

In the next chapter, we'll deal with something a little less scary and look at how you connect and manage USB and Bluetooth hardware devices on your PC, including printers and headphones.

CHAPTER 10

Connecting and Using Peripherals and Hardware

Do you still have a printer attached to your PC? These venerable devices are becoming less and less common, but many people still have one at home, and they're still pretty essential in the workplace. Let's face it, we might hardly use them these days, but there are still times when you really can't do without one.

Note If you are concerned about the carbon footprint associated with your use of printers in the home or workplace, you can find out how to become more sustainable with my book *The Green IT Guide (Apress, 2022)*.

Nowadays, we're more likely to attach Bluetooth headphones to our PCs, so we can watch streaming TV or play online games without disturbing anyone else in the household. It's not always a simple matter of plugging a USB cable into the PC or turning on your headphones though.

Sometimes the devices we want to use might argue with us, or Windows 11 might not realize that you actually *do* want to print from the printer you just plugged in, rather than the old one you had to throw away after it seized up. So, let's have a look at how we made sure all our devices behave themselves and work as we want them to.

Adding and Managing Printers

As we've been talking about printers, this seems like a good place to start. Windows 11 is pretty good at detecting printers plugged into your PC, or that are connected to your network via Wi-Fi, and installing them itself. Indeed, it's possible that when you come to install your printer, you could find it's already set up for you, which is a good thing.

© Mike Halsey 2022
M. Halsey, *Windows 11 Made Easy*, https://doi.org/10.1007/978-1-4842-8035-5_10

Installing a Printer in Windows 11

Let's assume though that you have to do so manually. To add a printer in Windows 11, open Settings and click *Bluetooth & devices* and then *Printers & scanners*. If you don't see your printer already in the list, click the *Add device* button, see Figure 10-1.

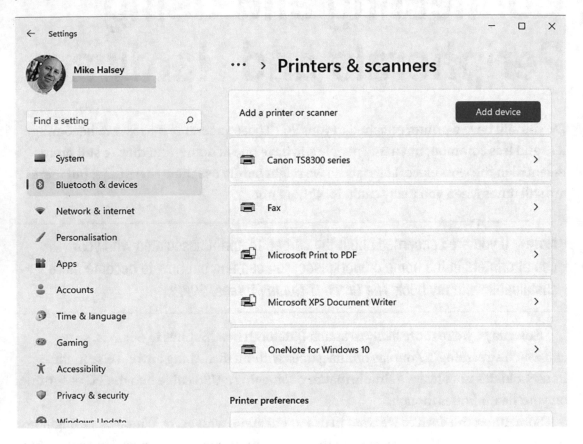

Figure 10-1. *Windows 11 makes it easy to add a printer*

Note   Before connecting a Wi-Fi printer, make sure you connect the printer to your Wi-Fi network (the same one as the PC) using its on-screen display or app.

Windows 11 will look for USB and Wi-Fi printers, and if it finds any, it will list them for you, but just in case it can't find the printer, it will also show you an *Add manually* link, see Figure 10-2, so let's have a look at this in case you need it.

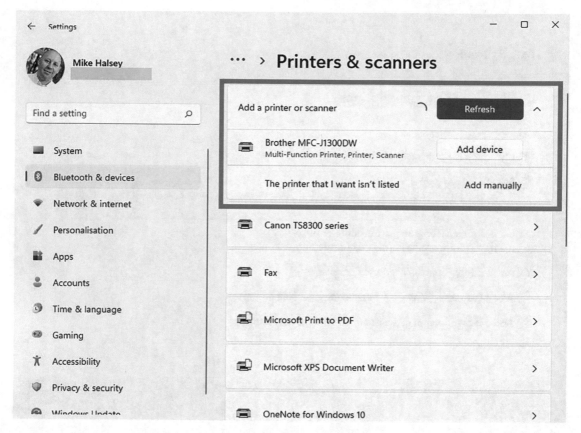

Figure 10-2. *Windows 11 will let you add a hard to find printer*

Clicking this link will display a new dialog with several options, see Figure 10-3. The first is called *My printer is a little older, help me find it,* and clicking this will make Windows 11 search again, but spend a little more time and expend a bit more effort in the search.

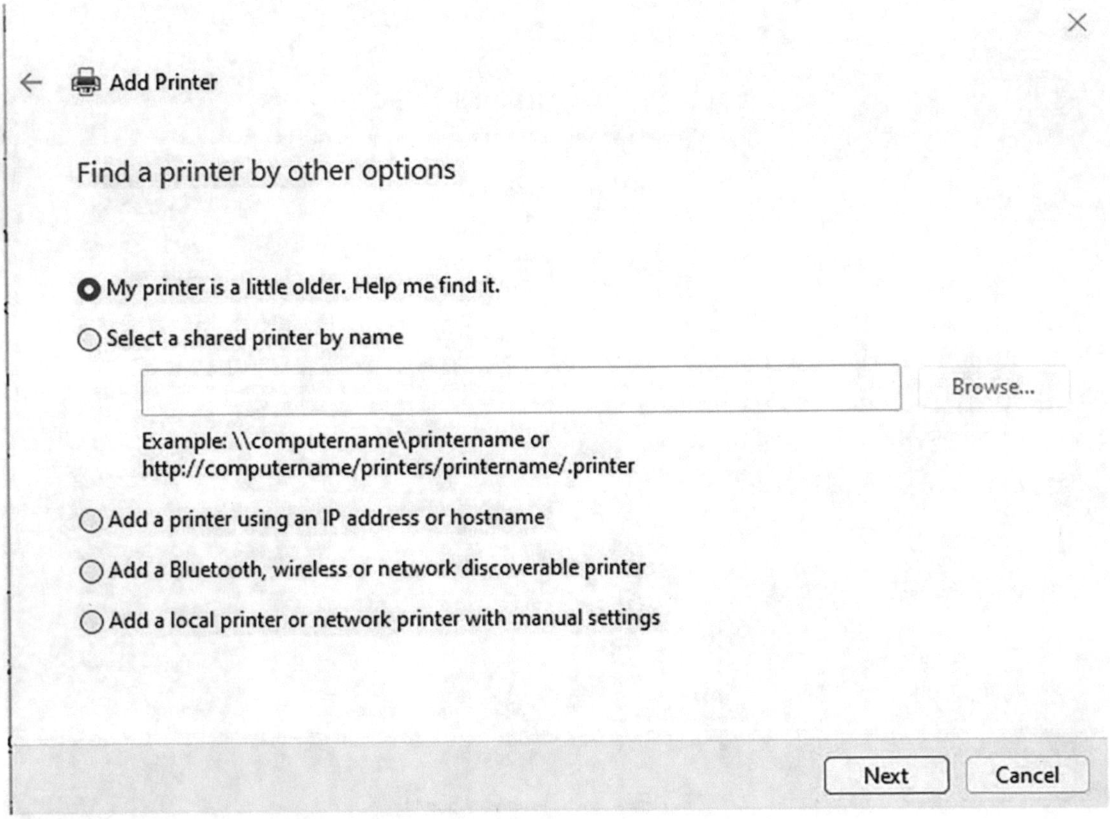

Figure 10-3. *Windows 11 lets you add a printer manually*

The second option is most useful when you are trying to connect to a printer in the workplace. Ask your system administrator for the "address" of the printer on the network. It will usually start with two forward slashes "\\". The same goes for the third option where your system administrator might give you the printer's IP address, which is the numerical device location on your network, not the location of the bathroom.

If you have a Bluetooth or a Wi-Fi printer that can't be found, then select the fourth option. The last option is only really to be used for much older parallel and serial printers, which are the connections we all used before USB was introduced in 1995. These printers are usually only still used for critical roles such as payroll.

Managing Printer Settings

If you click on a printer in the *Printers & scanners* Settings, you will see additional options for the printer. You may, but not always, see a *Set as default* button, see Figure 10-4, and there will also be a *Printing preferences* option.

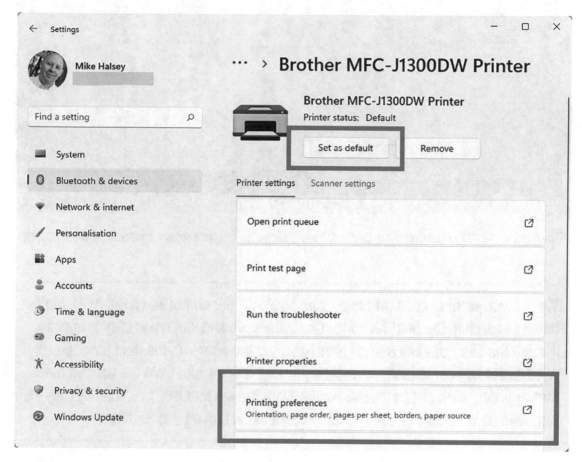

Figure 10-4. *You can configure a printer in Settings*

Opening the *Printer preferences* will display a dialog with options that your printer supports such as printing on both sides (to save paper), printing in draft mode or just in black and white (to save ink or toner), and printing on standard paper or photo paper. It's worth noting here that the dialog you see will vary depending on what printer you have installed, and you can see three such different dialogs in Figure 10-5.

Figure 10-5. *The dialog you see will vary depending on what printer you're using*

Tip   If you want to set a printer as your "default" but do not see a Set as Default button, search in the Start Menu for **Control Panel**, and when you click it to open it, click the *View devices and printers* link. Find the printer in the next panel you want to set as your default, right-click (tap and hold) it, and from the context menu that appears, click *Set as default printer*. Note though that this functionality may be removed as Windows 11 evolves and everything is moved into Settings.

Adding a Bluetooth Device

If your PC supports Bluetooth (and adding Bluetooth via a small USB dongle just costs a few dollars), then in the *Bluetooth & devices* Settings, you will see a big *Add device* button, see Figure 10-6.

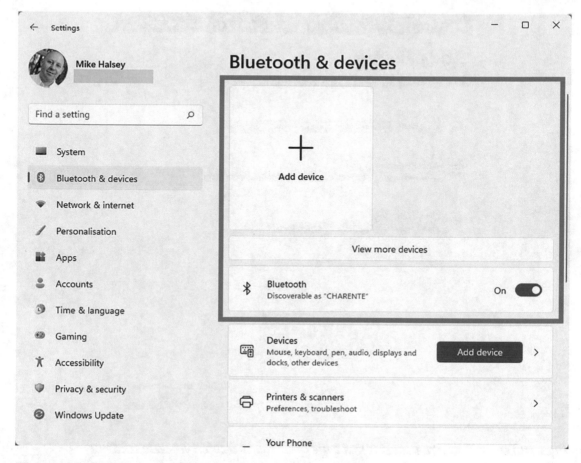

Figure 10-6. *You can add Bluetooth devices in Settings*

Note   Below the *Add device* button is an *on/off* switch for Bluetooth as while Bluetooth might be supported by your PC, it might be switched off.

You will be asked what type of device it is you want to add, see Figure 10-7. This includes *Bluetooth* devices (which include speakers, headphones, keyboards, and mice), a *Wireless display* (such as TV in the workplace for showing a presentation on), or *Everything else*, which is what you should click if you are adding an Xbox controller to your PC for gaming.

Figure 10-7. You are asked what type of wireless device you are adding

---

Note   Make sure the Bluetooth device is in "Pairing mode" before getting Windows 11 to search for it.

Windows 11 will then search for wireless devices and display any that it finds, see Figure 10-8. Some will connect automatically when you click them; others will require you to type a code or read a code from the device.

Figure 10-8. *Windows 11 will search for wireless devices*

Managing Problem Bluetooth Devices

Sometimes a Bluetooth device will simply not cooperate and won't reconnect when you want to use them. If this happens, you should remove the device and try reconnecting it. In the *Bluetooth & devices* Settings, click *Devices* and find the problem Bluetooth device in the list. Click the three vertical dots button to the right of its name, and then click *Remove device* from the menu that appears, see Figure 10-9. You can then try to reconnect the device.

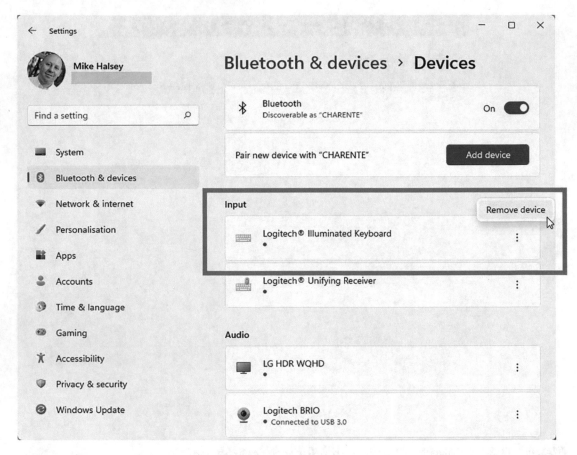

Figure 10-9. *Sometimes Bluetooth devices need to be removed and reattached*

Connecting to Other Devices in Your Home or Workplace

Occasionally you might want to connect your PC to another PC or device on your network. In Chapter 5, I showed how you can do this in File Explorer. Click *Network* in the left panel of File Explorer, and all available network computers and devices that Windows 11 can connect to will be displayed, see Figure 10-10.

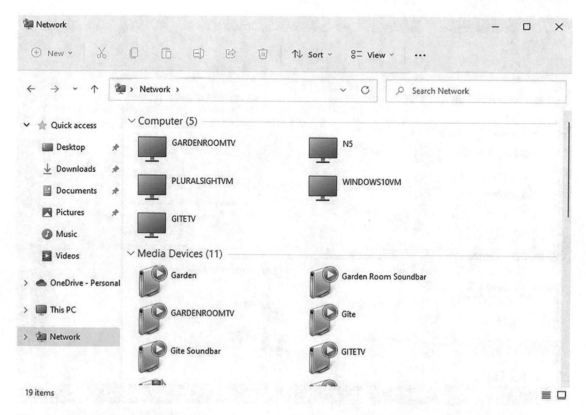

Figure 10-10. *You can connect to network devices and PCs in File Explorer*

There are a couple of useful additions though that can make your life a little simpler. Firstly, if you will need to access a device regularly, which is common for a network storage device such as a USB hard disk plugged into your Internet router or a network-attached storage (NAS) drive at your workplace, you can right-click on that device, and from the menu that appears, click *Pin to Quick access*. This will then pin a quick link to that device in the Quick Access panel on the left of File Explorer, see Figure 10-11.

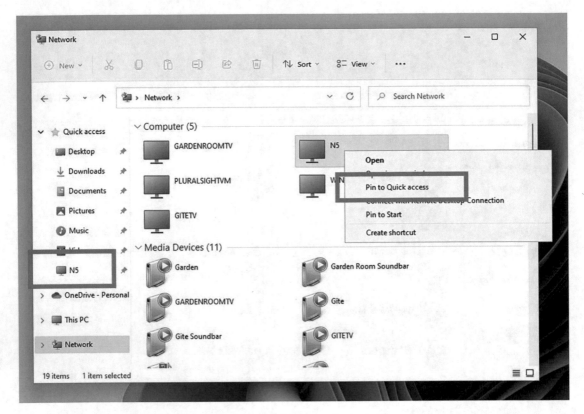

Figure 10-11. *You can pin a quick link to a network device in File Explorer*

You can later remove that quick link, by right-clicking it and selecting *Unpin* from the menu that appears.

If you need to connect to another PC on your network, or if a system administrator in your workplace needs to connect into your PC (always be careful who you give this permission to), open Settings, and in the *System* panel, scroll down until you see *Remote Desktop*. Click this and you will see a switch to turn *Remote Desktop* on or off, see Figure 10-12.

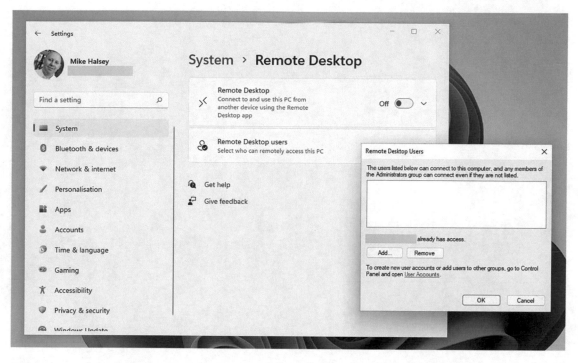

Figure 10-12. *Remote Desktop gives other people on other PCs access to your PC*

To give you additional peace of mind however, you can click *Remote Desktop users* and specify who can have access to the PC. This might be your partner or a colleague, and you can add them by typing the Microsoft Account or Azure AD account they sign into the network with, or by searching for their name on the company server.

Summary

Adding USB and Bluetooth devices to your PC is a simple and straightforward process in Windows 11, with the operating system doing much of the work for you. Managing those devices is equally straightforward, though as I mentioned a while ago, Bluetooth devices can sometimes put up a fight and need to be removed and reconnected.

In the next chapter, we'll look at more settings and how you can keep your copy of Windows 11 up to date with the latest security and stability patches and how you can defer annual feature updates for your PC.

CHAPTER 11

Keeping Your PC Updated and Running Smoothly

Nobody likes to have a PC that wants to restart to install updates during the day when you're in the middle of something. Whatever it is you're doing, be that shopping, reading, researching for college, working for your employer, or gaming, it's important and certainly far more important than Windows 11 wanting to "restart out of active hours," see Figure 11-1. If you can manage to do all your tasks during the correct hours, then surely your PC ought to be able to do the same.

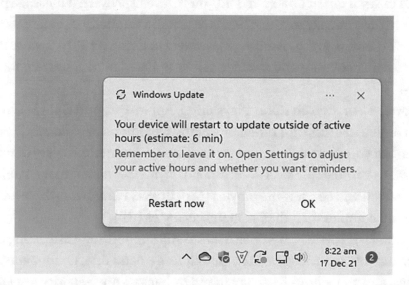

Figure 11-1. *It can be annoying when Windows wants to restart to install an update*

In truth, these PC restarts aren't anywhere near as common as they used to be, but they can still happen, and there are things you can do to try and prevent it.

© Mike Halsey 2022

M. Halsey, *Windows 11 Made Easy*, https://doi.org/10.1007/978-1-4842-8035-5_11

Why Windows Updates Are Important

When Microsoft launched Windows 10, they upset a lot of people by removing the ability to switch Windows Update off completely. It had been quite common with Windows XP and Windows 7 for people to do this, and I want to explain why Microsoft's stance was the right thing to do.

In Chapters 3 and 9, I've detailed the different types of threat that PC users face, from data mining to ransomware. It's important to understand that your PC isn't a consumer electronics device like your TV or fridge as it doesn't just do one job repetitively, and it's not isolated from the Internet. Yes, I know you'll use your TV to watch Netflix and YouTube, and these are online services, but what your TV is doing is interacting with just one or two websites and then only pulling content from them.

The connections to these websites will already be secured behind your personal accounts for them. What's more, if somebody wanted to attack the software on your TV, they'd likely need physical access to it as the operating systems they run on are proprietary and difficult for malware writers and hackers to target.

This isn't to say it doesn't happen, and you'll have likely seen a message pop up on your TV screen occasionally saying it needs to install an update or update its apps. Even our cars aren't immune to this, wanting to connect to home Wi-Fi to update themselves periodically so their software and security can be updated to help prevent them being stolen.

A Windows PC, or even an Xbox, Playstation, Apple iPad, and Google Chromebook are different as you use these for much more. You wouldn't type your credit card details into your car, but you do on a PC or games console, and sometimes very frequently.

Windows is a complex piece of code though. If you compare it to the banking app on your phone, which will be a few megabytes (MB) in size, Windows is thousands of times larger and more complex than that, at many gigabytes (GB).

But Windows isn't perfect. Because it has to still support software dating back almost 30 years, because big businesses and corporations demand this functionality, there are security holes, and sometimes these are found by hackers and security researchers. These holes need to be plugged.

Then there are new threats emerging all the time. Hackers and malware writers don't sit still. They're clever people and are always inventing new ways to attack computers, which is why even an iPad, with its completely locked-down ecosystem, is still vulnerable.

CHAPTER 11   KEEPING YOUR PC UPDATED AND RUNNING SMOOTHLY

All of this makes security and stability updates essential on all our devices, and so Microsoft's decision back in 2015 to make sure all Windows 10 and Windows 11 PCs get them was the right thing to do.

Using Windows Update

Generally speaking, Windows Update is one part of the operating system on your PC you should never need to visit. It just sits quietly in the background, doing its job and hopefully not getting in the way a lot. This doesn't mean a few tweaks can't improve the way it works for you.

You can find Windows Update in Settings by clicking *Windows Update* at the bottom of the left-side panel, see Figure 11-2. It will tell you if you are up to date, or if updates are available, and there's a big *Check for updates* button you can click to see if anything new is available.

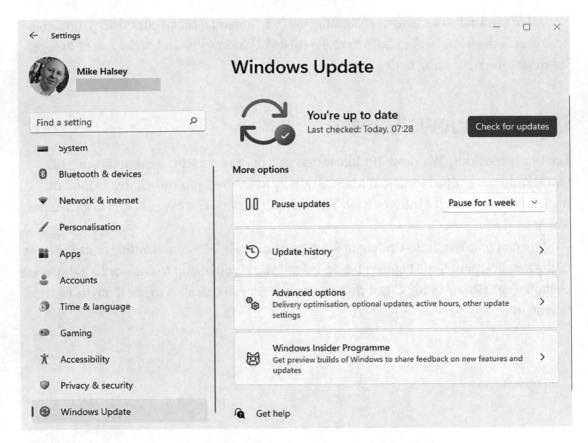

Figure 11-2.   *Windows Update can be found in Settings*

If you click *Advanced options*, then you can get finer control over how Windows Update works. At the top of the Advanced options page, you will see a switch to *Receive updates for other Microsoft products*, see Figure 11-3. This can be useful to check as it will help download security and stability updates for software including Microsoft Office and even Minecraft.

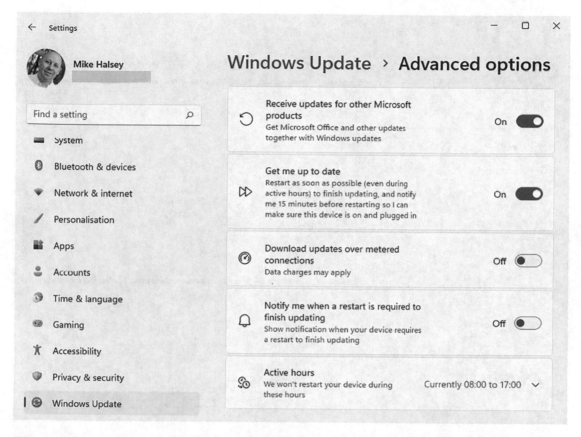

Figure 11-3. *Windows Update can download updates for other Microsoft products on your PC*

Setting Your Active Hours for PC Use

The *Get me up to date* option is one you might want to uncheck though, as this is the type of setting that will result in the "we need to restart your PC" notification we saw in Figure 11-1. This ties into the *Active hours* setting and this is something you might want to change.

You might, for example, typically use your PC late into the evening, or you could work nights, be an early-bird, or have any other reason to typically use your PC outside of the standard 8 a.m. to 5 p.m. hours. Clicking *Active hours* will therefore let you set the hours you typically use your PC manually or have Windows 11 watch how you use your PC for a while and then adjust them itself, see Figure 11-4.

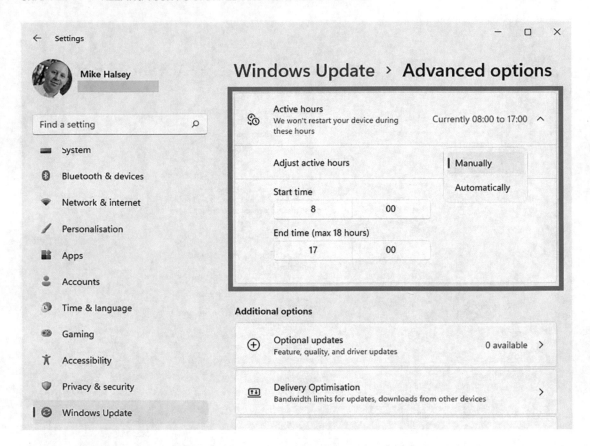

Figure 11-4. *You can tell Windows 11 when you normally use the PC*

If you use a laptop of tablet with a cellular modem installed, then you can optionally switch on *Download updates over metered connections*. Be careful with this however as cellular data can be expensive and Windows Updates can be large. That is why this option is disabled by default on your PC.

Tip   If you have a laptop or tablet and leave it in *Sleep* when you're not using it, Windows Update will typically wake it for a couple of minutes during the night to install any updates and perform any necessary restart, before putting it to sleep again.

Deferring and Pausing Updates

Sometimes you just don't want or need Windows 11 to be installing updates and pestering you to restart the PC. You might have an important work or college project to complete to deadline, and don't want interruptions, or the latest Call of Duty game might have just been released and you *really* don't want any interruptions.

Back at the main Windows Update settings, you will see an option called *Pause updates*. This has a drop-down menu to its right in which you can pause and defer updates for up to five weeks. This will prevent Windows from downloading anything that's not completely essential to keeping your PC secure, thus minimizing any potential disruption to your work, see Figure 11-5.

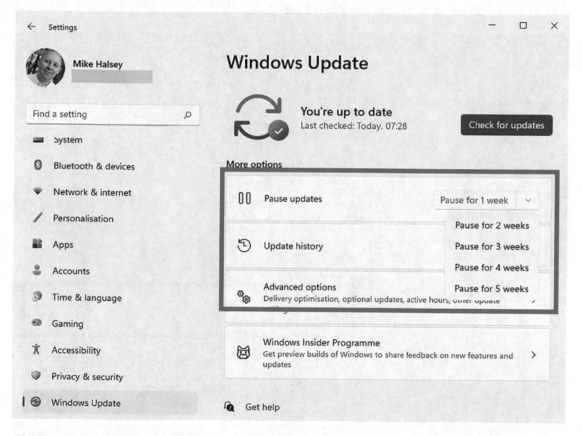

Figure 11-5. *You can tell Windows 11 to pause updates for up to five weeks*

Uninstalling Problematic Updates

It's not just updates for Windows 11 and Microsoft Office that come through Windows update. You will often find driver updates for your hardware and graphics card being delivered this way too. Sometimes though you might find a Windows Update causing problems on a PC, and you want to remove it.

This is relatively easily done in Windows 11. I say relatively because not all updates can be removed, what Microsoft classes as important security and stability updates can't be removed in this way.

In the main Windows Update Settings, click *Update History* and then scroll to the very bottom of that page. You will see an *Uninstall updates* option, see Figure 11-6. Click this to see what updates can be removed from your PC.

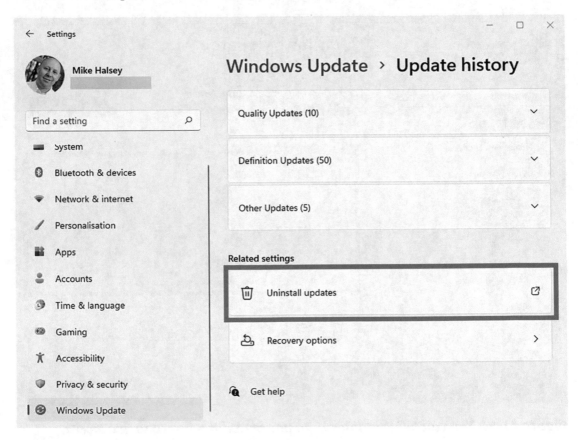

Figure 11-6. *You can remove (uninstall) some updates from your PC*

This will open a new window listing all the updates that can be uninstalled from your PC. To the right of each one is the date on which it was installed. It can be almost impossible to tell from the names of updates what they were, but you can likely tie the install date to the point where your problems began, to help you identify which one to remove, see Figure 11-7.

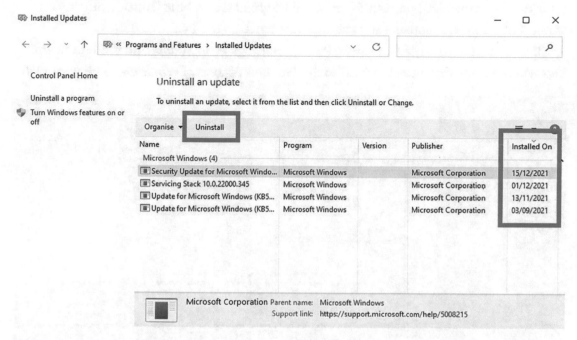

Figure 11-7. *Windows 11 lets you uninstall some, but not all, updates*

Once you have identified the update you want to uninstall, click or touch it to select it, and an *Uninstall* button will appear in the toolbar just above it. You can click this to remove the update.

Note   This functionality is something I am expecting to change over time, with this older *Control Panel* window being folded completely into Settings. What you see might therefore vary from what I've detailed but the core functionality won't change very much, if at all.

Uninstalling Windows Feature Packs

Windows Feature Packs are delivered once a year and include new features and updates for the operating system. They typically come in the autumn (fall) and sometimes, very occasionally, can bring a few bugs and problems with them. You'll know when a feature pack has been installed on your PC as you'll be greeted by a blue "introducing the new version of Windows" screen the next time you sign into the PC.

If you need to uninstall a Feature Pack, in Settings go to *System* and then *Recovery*. You will then see an option to revert to the *Previous version of Windows*, see Figure 11-8.

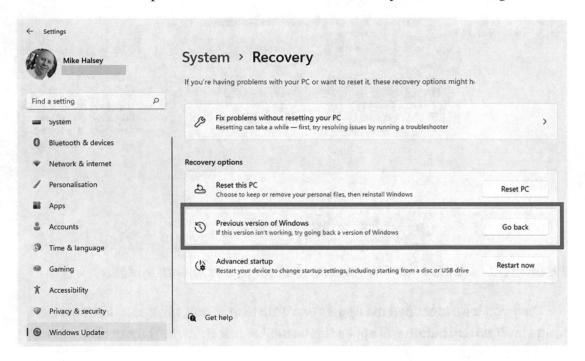

Figure 11-8. *Windows lets you uninstall a Feature Pack up to 30 days after it was installed*

Windows keeps a backup copy of your previous version (how your PC was before the Feature Pack was installed) for 30 days after the new installation. Within this time, you can uninstall the Feature Pack. I then recommend that you defer updates as I detailed earlier in this chapter for a few weeks to give Microsoft time to sort out any bugs and problems before you download it again.

If a Windows Update Makes Your PC Unstable

This circumstance is extremely rare and is most likely to be caused by a poorly written hardware driver being delivered through Windows Update, but if you ever find that your PC becomes unstable or maybe even unable to start, you can still remove the offending update, roll back to how things were before, and then *Defer* updates as I detailed earlier in this chapter until Microsoft or the hardware driver provider has had time to sort things out.

You can do this by using *System Restore*, and I will detail how you can use this in Chapter 12. I also recommend you create a *USB Recovery Drive*, which I also detail in Chapter 12, just in case an update or another problem means your PC is unable to start to the desktop.

Introducing the Windows Insider Program

Some people are PC enthusiasts, and not content with just using the current build of Windows 11, they want to see what's coming next. For this, Microsoft have created the *Windows Insider Program*. This is a way for your PC to get advance (beta) builds of the next updates to Windows 11 (and Windows 12 when that likely comes along in a few years).

Caution   Beta builds of Windows 11 can be unstable or have functionality you need that doesn't work properly. It is unwise to install these builds on your primary PC, or one you rely on to work, shop, or bank.

You can sign up for the Windows Insider Program in Windows Update where you will see a link for it. You will see a message saying that this will enable you to "try new features before they release and give feedback." If you want to join, click the *Get started* button.

You will be asked what "Channel" of the Insider Program you want to join, see Figure 11-9. These all give you different builds of Windows, and some of those builds will be more stable and reliable than others.

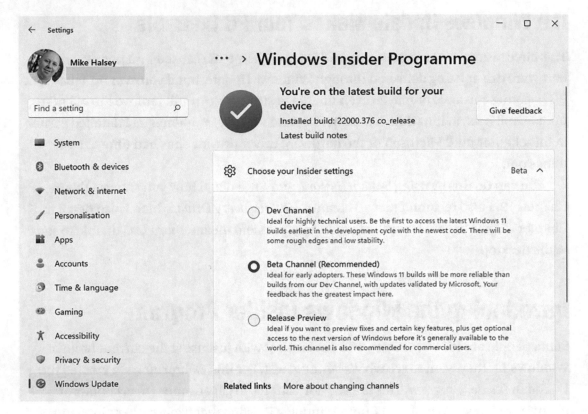

Figure 11-9. *The Windows Insider Program has three "channels"*

- **Dev Channel** otherwise called the "developer channel" is where you will receive the earliest and therefore the least stable builds. You should only sign up for this channel if you are a true enthusiast that knows what you're doing with PCs.

- **Beta Channel** is the main channel for seeing new features early and will also include much more stable builds than the Dev channel.

- **Release Preview** is where you will get early access to the next Feature Pack for Windows. These releases don't come along very often as Feature Packs are only released once a year.

If you want to stop getting preview builds of Windows, in the Windows Insider Program settings, you can check the box to *Stop getting preview builds*, see Figure 11-10. This will unenroll you from the program automatically when the next major version of Windows 11 or Feature Pack is released.

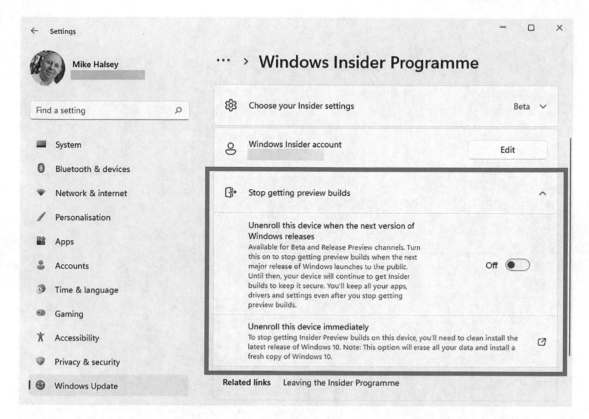

Figure 11-10. *You can stop getting preview builds if and when you choose*

I don't recommend that you choose the *Unenroll this device immediately* as you will then need to completely reinstall Windows 11 and all your apps and accounts. Should this become necessary for you though, you can download a fresh installer for Windows 11 from the Microsoft website at `www.microsoft.com/software-download/windows11`.

Summary

It's fairly straightforward to keep Windows Update under control if you find that it's annoying you. If, however, you haven't really noticed it, then you'll be completely fine leaving it alone and letting it get on with updating, protecting, and securing your PC.

We've only got one chapter left to go now, so I want to share with you my top-tips for getting the very best from both Windows 11 and your experience with your PC, including how you can use keyboard and trackpad shortcuts to be more productive, to ways you can repair problems with Windows 11 should they occur.

CHAPTER 12

Top Tips for Getting the Very Best from Windows 11

Throughout this book I've shown you how to get the very best experience from using Windows 11 on your PC, including how to keep yourself and your family safe, how to be productive and work from home, and how to make Windows 11 easier to use and more accessible. But there's still more benefit you can get from Windows 11, so in this chapter, I want to share with you my very best top-tips for getting the best from Windows 11 on your PC.

Using Keyboard Shortcuts with Windows 11

In Chapter 5, I showed you how you can get started with keyboard shortcuts in Windows 11, but using *Ctrl + X* (cut), *Ctrl + C* (copy), and *Ctrl + V* (paste) when working with files and documents, and indeed these shortcuts can also be used with text, images, and other content within your documents.

There are many more keyboard shortcuts you can use though that can make your life simpler, and here I want to share my favorites with you. Let's start with general keyboard shortcuts (Table 12-1).

© Mike Halsey 2022
M. Halsey, *Windows 11 Made Easy*, https://doi.org/10.1007/978-1-4842-8035-5_12

Table 12-1. *Windows 11 keyboard shortcuts*

Press this...	To do this...
Ctrl + Z	Undo the last action
Alt + Tab	Switch between open apps
Alt + F4	Close the active item or the open app
F2	Rename the current item (File Explorer)
F3	Open search (File Explorer)
F5	Refresh the open window (F9 in Microsoft Outlook)
F10	Activate the menu bar in the current app
Alt + F8	Show your password on the sign-in screen
Alt + Left/right arrow	Go back/forward
Alt + Page up/down	Move up/down one screen
Ctrl + A	Select all items
Ctrl + Y	Redo an action that was previously undone
Ctrl + Left/right arrow	Move one word left or right
Ctrl + Up/down arrow	Move to beginning/end of paragraph
Ctrl + Shift + Esc	Open Task Manager
Windows key + A	Open Quick Settings
Windows key + C	Open Microsoft Teams Chat
Windows key + D	Minimize / Restore all windows on the desktop
Windows key + E	Open File Explorer
Windows key + G	Open Xbox Game Bar
Windows key + I	Open Settings
Windows key + L	Lock your PC
Windows key + N	Open Notification center
Windows key + R	Open the Run dialog
Windows key + S	Open Search

(continued)

Table 12-1. (*continued*)

Press this...	To do this...
Windows key + U	Open Accessibility settings
Windows key + V	Open the clipboard history
Windows key + W	Open the Widgets
Windows key + Z	Open Snap layouts
Windows key + . (Period)	Open the Emoji panel
Windows key + Tab	Open Task View
Windows key + PrtScn	Save a screenshot to a file

These are not the complete list of keyboard shortcuts in Windows, and if you want to learn more, you can find the complete list on the Microsoft website at https://pcs.tv/3J4FXLI.

Using Touch and Trackpad Gestures with Windows 11

If you use a laptop or a PC with a touchscreen, you can also achieve more by using simple gestures. Table 12-2 shows what you can do.

Table 12-2. *Windows 11 trackpad gestures*

Action	Gestures
Scroll	Slide two fingers up or down
Zoom in or out	Pinch in or out with two fingers
Show more commands (right-click)	Press and hold
Open all windows	Swipe three fingers upward
Minimize all windows	Swipe three fingers downward
Switch between open apps	Swipe three fingers left or right
Open Notification center	Swipe one finger from the right edge
Open Widgets	Swipe one finger from the left edge
Switch desktops	Swipe four fingers left or right

Again, Microsoft have a complete list available on their website which you can find on this link `https://pcs.tv/3yuKjXB`.

Maximize Your Laptop or Tablet's Battery Life

In my book, *The Green IT Guide (Apress, 2022)*, I write a lot about how businesses, organizations, and individuals can make their computer use more sustainable and environmentally friendly. One part of that is all of us using less electricity, and one part of that is making your laptop or tablet's battery last longer on a single charge.

This is a great idea anyway as it means you can work for longer away from your charger, and in Windows 11, it's simple to make some changes to optimize your power use.

Tip   Did you know it uses more power to start an app than to leave it running? Minimizing your open apps that you will need later will use less power than closing them completely.

In Settings, under *System* click *Power & battery*, you will see various options for managing power usage on your laptop. These include changing after how many minutes of inactivity the screen turns off and when the laptop goes to sleep.

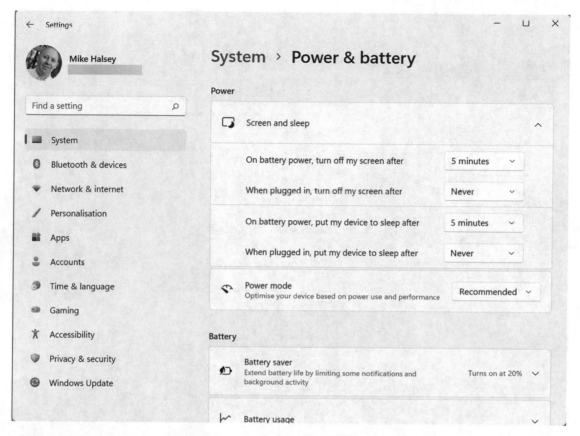

Figure 12-1. *You can change power settings for a laptop or tablet*

Tip   Windows 11 laptops and tablets resume from sleep in just a couple of seconds and use very little power when in a sleep state. This is much more power-efficient than shutting down and restarting the PC.

There are also Battery saver settings, and you can set at which percentage of remaining battery these kick in, see Figure 12-2. Battery Saver limits background tasks such as downloading updates or auto-checking email, to save power usage.

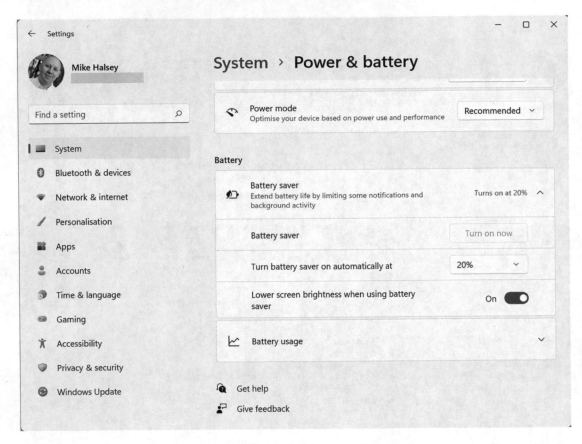

Figure 12-2. *Battery Saver limits some background tasks to save power*

Tip   The biggest power hog on any PC is the screen. Lowering your screen's brightness from full to 70% can have a dramatically positive effect on battery life, while still leaving the screen very legible.

Repurposing an Old PC to Sell or Donate

While we're on the subject of sustainability and being environmentally friendly, the amount of dangerous chemicals and metals that go into making modern electronics is scary, and plastics can only be recycled about five times before we have no choice but to send them to landfill.

If you have an older PC that you don't need anymore, it's a good idea to think if it can be sold or given to a friend, colleague, or family member instead of going in the ever-growing e-waste pile.

You can completely wipe a PC of all your installed apps, documents and files, and user accounts in Settings. Navigate to *System ➤ Recovery* and you will see a *Reset this PC* option, see Figure 12-3. Click this and you will see a *Remove everything* option that will rest your PC so it can be sold or donated.

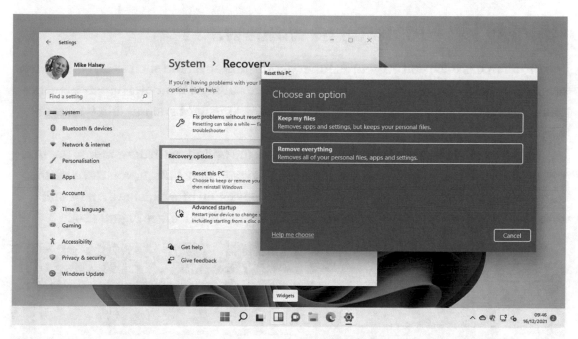

Figure 12-3. *You can reset a PC so it can be sold or donated*

Tip   *Reset* is also available in Windows 10 and can be found in *Settings ➤ Update & security ➤ Recovery.*

One thing I mention in *The Green IT Guide* is that if you would rather donate an old PC to charity, there are many local, national, and international charities in your city, state, or country that will repurpose them and give them to low-income families or developing countries. A search online can help you find repurposing schemes in your area.

Caution   *Reset* will delete files from a PC, but it won't do it securely, so with the right tools, they could later be recovered. To completely and securely wipe the free space on a PC (after you have deleted your files and documents), download free software such as the venerable CCleaner from `www.ccleaner.com`.

Quickly Fix Problems in Windows 11

If a problem has occurred on your PC after performing an action such as installing a new app, a new hardware driver, or downloading and installing a Windows update or feature pack, a system exists to help you quickly roll back the changes and put things back the way they were before.

In the Start Menu, search for *Restore* and click the option to *Create a restore point*. A dialog will appear in which you (should) see a *System Restore* button, you can click this, and you can choose from available saved restore points, all of which have a date and time to help you select one before the recent change took place, see Figure 12-4.

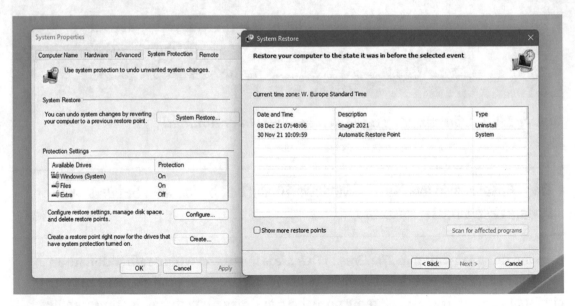

Figure 12-4. *System Restore lets you roll back changes made to a PC*

If the *System Restore* button is greyed-out, click the *Configure* button and then select *Turn on system protection*. Windows 11 will now start keeping restore points. It can be worth checking this early on, just in case you get a problem later.

Create a USB Recovery Drive

While we're on the subject of System Restore, there's nothing more annoying than having a PC that won't start to the desktop. Very occasionally a problem might occur that's serious enough for this to happen. To help with this, you can create a USB Recovery drive that you can keep safe in case you need it later.

In the Start Menu, search for *recovery* and click *Recovery drive* when it appears in the search results. A dialog will appear asking if you also want to include a backup copy of Windows 11, "Back up system files...", see Figure 12-5. This is optional but can't do any harm if you ever need to reinstall Windows 11 later.

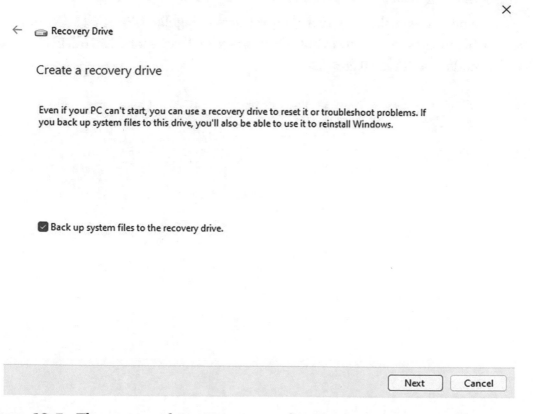

Figure 12-5. *The recovery drive creator runs from an easy-to-use wizard*

You'll need to plug in a USB drive that is at least 16GB (gigabytes) in size, though that's small by today's standards, so you won't have trouble finding a cheap one of that size or larger. Then click *Next* start creating the drive.

If your PC won't start to the desktop and doesn't automatically go into the *Recovery options* which I will talk about in a moment, plug the USB Recovery drive into the PC and start it from that. Note that you might need to press the **F8** key a few times as your PC starts to display the option to boot the PC from USB.

When you are in the Recovery options, Windows might try an auto-repair. If this fails to work, you will see additional options. Here you can click *Troubleshoot,* and then at the next screen, click *Advanced options* to display the options you need.

Note   If you want to restore a backup of Windows 11 stored on your USB Recovery Drive, click *Use a device* from the first screen, and then select the USB drive from the list of devices that appear.

On the next screen, there are two options I want to highlight. The first is System Restore which works identically to how I have described earlier and can roll back recent changes made to a PC, see Figure 12-6.

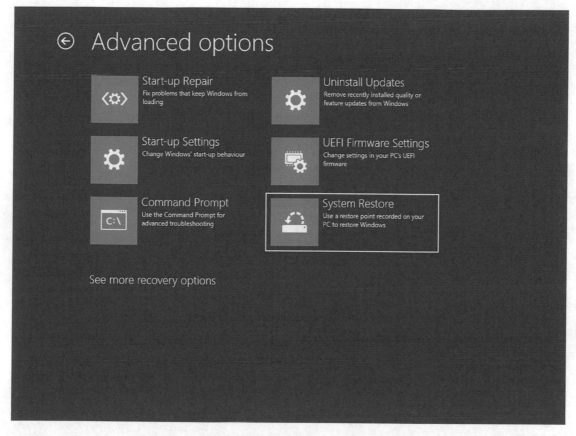

Figure 12-6. *You can run System Restore from a USB Recovery Drive*

You will also see an *Uninstall updates* option, and you can click this to remove recent Windows Updates if one has caused the PC to become unstable.

Get Help from, or Give Help to a Friend

If you sign into your PC using a Microsoft Account or a workplace Azure AD account, you can use a feature called *Quick Assist* to see and control another PC remotely over the Internet, and it works very effectively. In the Start Menu, search for *quick* and run Quick Assist when it appears in the Search Results.

You will be asked if you want to *Get assistance* from someone else, or to *Give assistance*, see Figure 12-7. The person giving assistance will be given a six-digit code that the person getting assistance needs to type into the Quick Assist window.

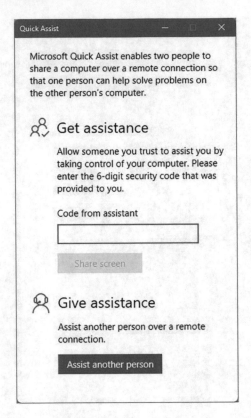

Figure 12-7. *Quick Assist is useful for helping someone on another PC remotely*

With this done the person giving assistance will be asked if they want to take full control of the PC, or just view the screen. The person receiving assistance needs to authorize control being given.

Caution   Always be careful who you give control of your PC to, if for example you get an email or a telephone call claiming to be from Microsoft or a security company saying that malware has been identified on your PC it will **ALWAYS** be a scam!

The person giving assistance will then be able to see, and optionally control, the remote PC. In the top-right corner of the Quick Assist screen-sharing window is a three dots menu button that lets you choose various options, such as viewing the remote screen full size, switch between multiple monitors on the remote PC, and end the support session, see Figure 12-8.

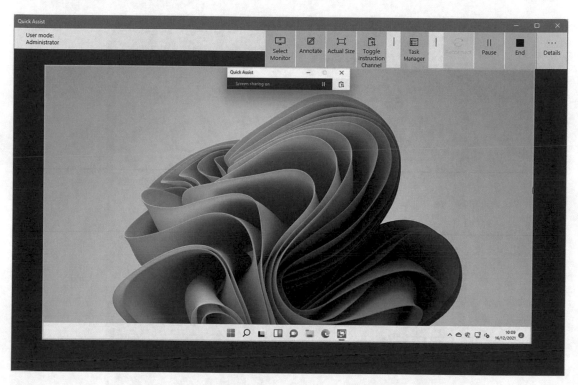

Figure 12-8. The person giving support can see and control the remote PC

Reset Your Wi-Fi or Network Settings

Sometimes you might encounter a problem with a Wi-Fi network, or your networking settings might become corrupt, stopping you from getting online. There are two things you can do here.

If you can't connect to a Wi-Fi network, then it's possible the settings on your PC for that Wi-Fi network have become corrupt. Open *Quick Settings* and click the arrow to the right of the Wi-Fi icon. This will display a list of current Wi-Fi networks, and you can right-click the offending network and click *Forget* from the options that appear, see Figure 12-9.

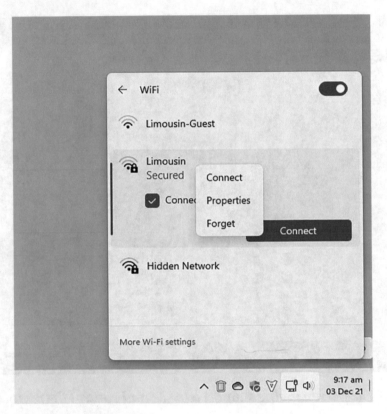

Figure 12-9. *You can tell Windows 11 to forget a Wi-Fi network*

The next time you connect to this network, it will be as though it's for the first time, though bear in mind you will need to reenter the access password if there is one.

Networking Settings Reset

If all of your network settings appear to have gone wonko, you can reset it all very easily. In Settings, navigate to *Network & internet* and then *Advanced network settings*. Here you will see a button called *Network reset*, see Figure 12-10.

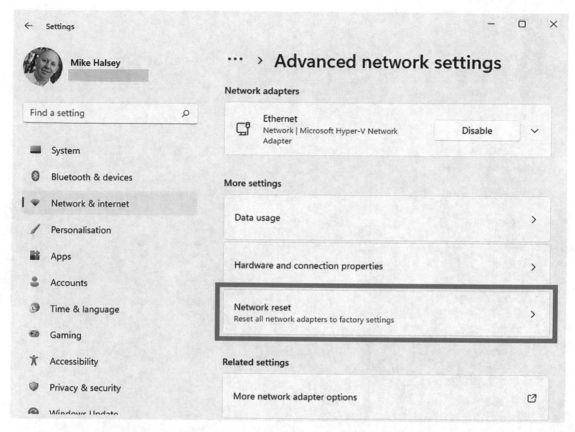

Figure 12-10. *You can reset all your networking settings in Windows 11*

Network reset will restore all of your PC's networking settings to their default (factory) state, and this can very often get your networking working again on the PC.

The Windows 11 Troubleshooters

Speaking of Windows 11 fixing problems on its own, in Settings if you go to *System*, then *Troubleshoot*, and *Other trouble-shooters*, you will find a list of troubleshooters built into the operating system, see Figure 12-11.

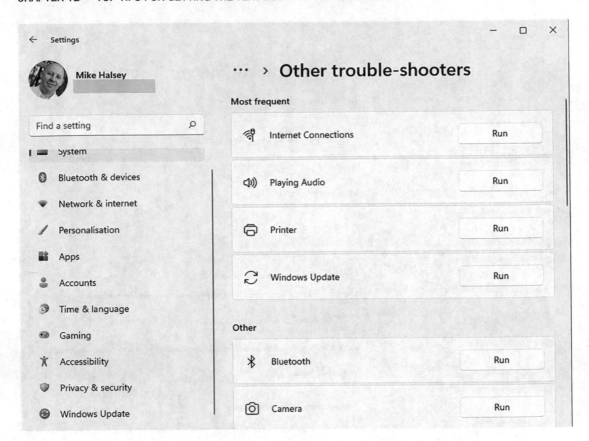

Figure 12-11. *Windows 11 include many troubleshooting tools*

All of these troubleshooters, which include audio, printers, Bluetooth, power, apps, and more, will reset Windows 11 components to their default state. This can, in all honesty, fix problems more times than you might realize; they're useful to run if you encounter a problem.

Stop Apps from Starting with Windows

Sometimes you will install an app that just insists on starting every time you turn on your PC, but you don't want it to, because you only use it occasionally. This is easily fixed. *Right-click* the Start button on the Taskbar and from the menu that appears click *Task Manager*. Then click the *More details* button in the bottom-left corner of the window that appears.

You will now see the full Windows Task Manager, which is usually used for seeing what apps are running, and for closing ones that have crashed or are causing a problem (which you can do under the *Processes* tab by right-clicking them).

Navigate to the *Startup* tab and you will see a list of apps that start automatically with Windows 11, see Figure 12-12. You will see if they are currently enabled or disabled and what their "start-up impact" is, that is, how much if at all they slow the PC.

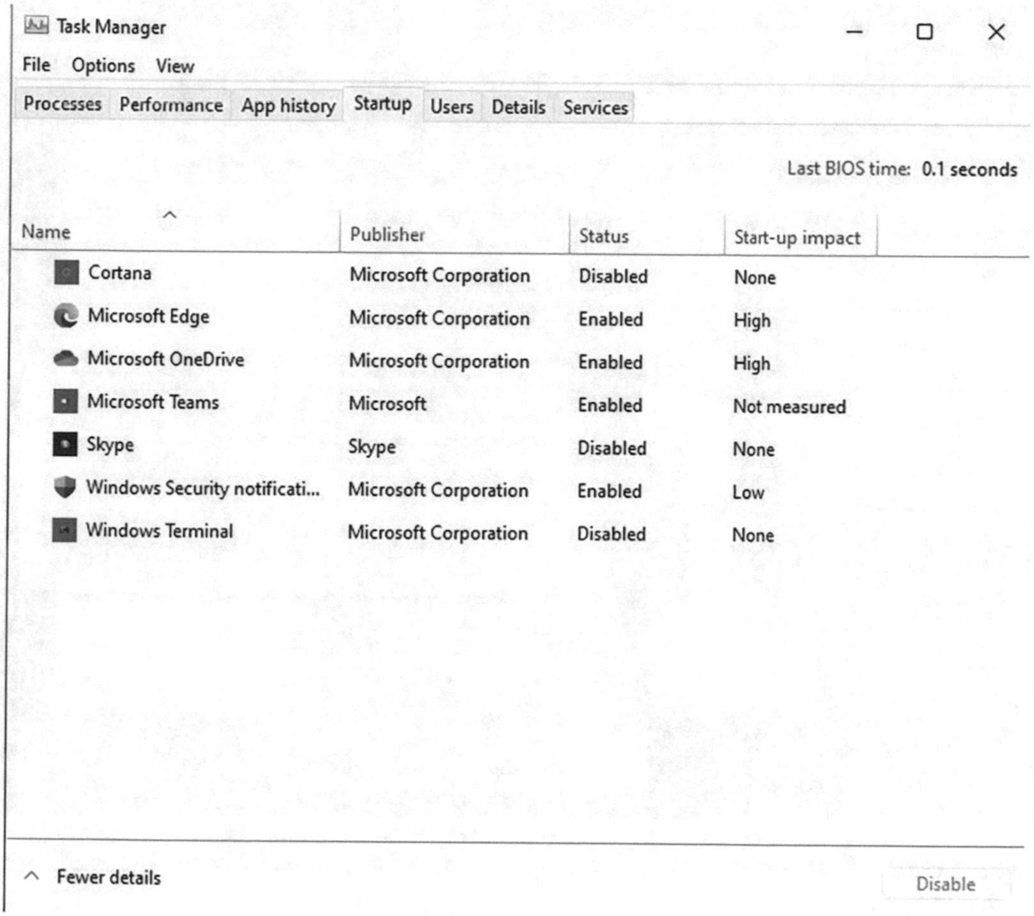
Task Manager
File Options View
Processes Performance App history Startup Users Details Services
Last BIOS time: 0.1 seconds
Name
Publisher
Status
Start-up impact
Cortana
Microsoft Corporation
Disabled
None
Microsoft Edge
Microsoft Corporation
Enabled
High
Microsoft OneDrive
Microsoft Corporation
Enabled
High
Microsoft Teams
Microsoft
Enabled
Not measured
Skype
Skype
Disabled
None
Windows Security notificati...
Microsoft Corporation
Enabled
Low
Windows Terminal
Microsoft Corporation
Disabled
None
Fewer details
Disable

Figure 12-12. *You can disable start-up apps in Windows 11*

If you want to disable an app from starting when you turn your PC on, or perhaps re-enable one that was previously disabled, then click it, and a *Disable/Enable* button will become available in the bottom-right corner of the window.

Choose What Apps Open Files and Documents

Sometimes you want to open a file or document using a specific app, but when you double-click the file, it opens in a different app instead. You can fix this by right-clicking on the file or document in File Explorer and from the menu that appears click *Open with*, see Figure 12-13.

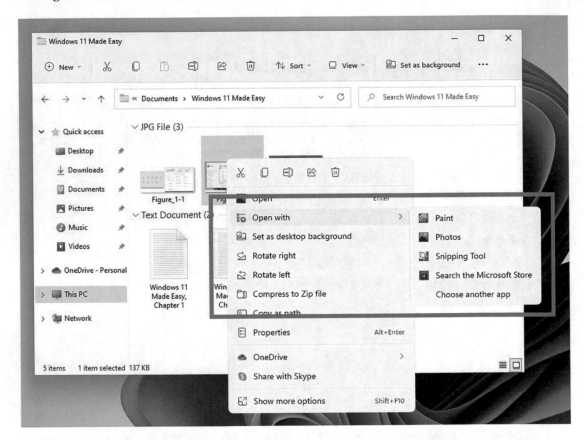

Figure 12-13. *You can choose what apps are used to open different types of files and documents*

This will display a menu listing different apps that can open that type of file. If you want to permanently change what app opens that file type though, click *Choose another app*. This will display a new dialog in which you can choose from one of the listed apps or search for a new app in the Microsoft store.

If you click the *More apps* link, you will also see an option to *Look for another app on this PC* which will let you search for a specific app. You can then check the box to *Always use this app to open...* that file type and press *OK*, see Figure 12-14.

Figure 12-14. *You can tell Windows 11 to always use a specific app to open a file or document type*

Change the Audio Device in Windows

Sometimes you might find your audio is coming out of the wrong device, perhaps because you have just plugged in a new monitor that has its own included speakers. This is very easy to fix. Open *Quick settings* and then click the arrow to the right of the volume slider control, see Figure 12-15.

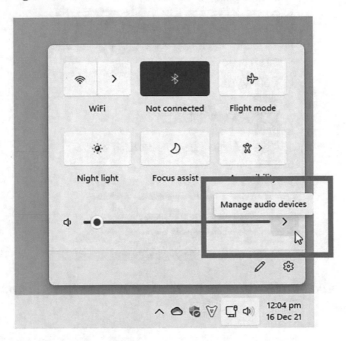

Figure 12-15. *You can switch between audio devices in Quick Settings*

You will now see a list of available audio devices, see Figure 12-16. To switch to a different audio device, simply click its name.

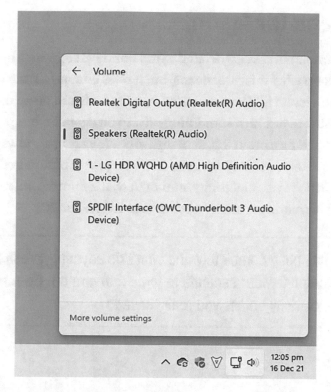

Figure 12-16. *You can easily choose a different audio device*

Plug It into a Different USB Port

A few years ago, while writing another book that was being peer-reviewed by an engineer on the Windows team at Microsoft, I got into a bit of an argument. I had included that if you found your printer, or another USB device, wasn't working, you should unplug it and then plug it into a different USB port. This would, you might have to try two or three ports, force Windows to reinstall the driver for the device and get it working again.

The engineer argued that this wasn't a problem in Windows as Microsoft had never heard of it. I stood my ground and the tip stayed in the book, as it is here too. So, if you have a problem with a USB device not working, don't listen to Microsoft, just plug it into a different USB socket.

Turn It Off and On Again!

There are two common phrases associated with IT and PC support. The first is RTFM, and I'll let you look up what this one means, but it does contain a rude word so I won't include it here. The second is "Have you tried turning it off and on again?"

It might seem silly to just turn something off and on again to fix a problem, but you might be surprised just how often this actually works. My advice is always to switch something off completely (select *Shut down* from the power button in the Start Menu), perhaps unplug it from mains electricity, and then wait a minute and restart it. This works equally well for hardware such as printers as it does for PCs.

Tip   If your PC has hung completely and won't do anything, press and hold the physical power button for four seconds to force it to turn off. **Do not** just unplug it from the mains electricity unless you really have to.

Summary

There are a lot of tips and hints you can find online about Windows and PCs, but these are by far my favorites. You can find many more Windows 11 hints and tips though on my own website, `Windows.do`. I would recommend you bookmark this site as I add new hints and tips on a regular basis.

This book was originally supposed to be about 100 pages shorter than it turned out to be, but I just couldn't help myself, as there's so much cool stuff in Windows 11 that you can use to have fun, get stuff done, solve problems, and more that it just all had to be included.

As regards the troubleshooting information in this chapter, if you feel you're competent with fixing Windows problems and want to learn more about it, then my next book after this will be *Windows 11 Troubleshooting (Apress, 2022)*, so you might want to look out for it.

Don't forget that Windows 11 will change over time, as Windows 10 did, so some things such as the Settings panel might look slightly different than the images I've included here. The broad functionality will always remain though, and both the Start Menu and Settings have search boxes which you can use to find what you need.

So, for now, I hope you have fun using your Windows 11 PC and that this book has helped you get more enjoyment from doing so. Many thanks for taking the time to read it.

Index

A

Accessibility options
    control panel, 120
    dictate text and commands, 120
    features, 115, 116
    keyboard/mouse, 118, 119
    lock screen, 113, 114
    mouse pointer, 118, 119
    quick settings menu, 115
    settings options, 116, 117
    voice typing, 120, 121
Android apps
    installation, 86, 87
    settings links, 88, 89
    start menu, 87, 88
Audio device, 235, 236

B, C, D

Battery Saver limits, 220–222
Bluetooth device
    remove device, 195, 196
    settings panel, 192, 193
    wireless devices, 193–195

E

Easier-see
    accessibility (*see* Accessibility options)
    color-blind, 125
    hearing option, 126–128
    high-contrast theme, 125, 126

    immersive reader button, 123
    magnifier, 124, 125
    narrator, 123
    scale option, 121, 122
    text reader, 122
    visual effects, 123
    visual notification options, 127

F, G

File Explorer
    breadcrumb bar, 104, 105
    files/folders, 98, 99
    folders/disk folders, 106
    multiple files, 94, 95
    network storage, 103, 104
    OneDrive (*see* OneDrive apps)
    opening/controlling files, 99, 100
    personalization, 101, 102
    present files
        flat files, 95, 96
        folders button, 97, 98
        group by option, 96, 97
    search options, 100, 101
    technical disk and folder, 105
    view and access remote storage, 103
    window options, 93
Files/documents, 232, 233

H

Hybrid-working, 151

© Mike Halsey 2022
M. Halsey, *Windows 11 Made Easy*, https://doi.org/10.1007/978-1-4842-8035-5

Snap layouts (*cont.*)

multiple-monitor representation,
138, 139

representation, 137

resolution/screen size, 136

drag and drop windows, 135

focus assist, 149, 150

layout options, 130

multiple desktops, 133–135

PDF (*see* Portable Document
Format (PDF))

pen/ink options, 142–145

resize apps, 131, 132

sticky notes app, 146–148

task view button, 133

whiteboard space, 145, 146

window layout, 129

Start-up apps, 231, 232

Store

Android apps, 86–89

gaming library, 84

Microsoft Store (*see* Microsoft Store)

third-party stores, 84, 85

traditional apps, 91

uninstall option, 89–91

Xbox Game Bar, 91, 92

System restore, 222, 223

T

Trackpad gestures/touchscreen, 217, 218

Troubleshooters, 229, 230

Two-factor authentication (TFA), 166, 167

U, V

USB device, 235

USB recovery drive, 223–225

W

Wi-Fi network

advanced network settings, 228, 229

cellular networks, 53

menu option, 51, 52

password screen, 51

properties/additional options, 52

quick settings panel, 50

reset options, 228

Windows 11

desktop/start menu, 6

document used, 11

evolution, 2

feature pack, 3

files/documents

file explorer panel, 20

file selection, 22

sort and view buttons, 21

learning process, 1

local accounts, 3–5

lock screen, 5, 6

Microsoft system, 3

notifications, 7, 8, 22–24

pinned and installed apps, 9, 10

quick settings panel, 24, 25

restart menu, 11, 12

running/finding apps

apps view, 14

Microsoft Store, 14, 15

mouse/finger, 12, 13

searching option, 15, 16

settings panel, 2

start menu, 8, 9

switching device, 25–27

system tray sits, 7

taskbar icons, 7

touch screen device, 16–19

X, Y, Z

Printed in the United States
by Baker & Taylor Publisher Services